MEDITATION AND MODERN PSYCHOLOGY

ROBERT ORNSTEIN

MALOR BOOKS

This is a Malor Books publication
An imprint of ISHK
PO Box 176, Los Altos, CA 94023

The original title of this work, *The Techniques of Meditation and their Implications for Modern Psychology* was published in *On the Psychology of Meditation* by Claudio Naranjo and Robert Ornstein ©1971 by Viking Compass

This Edition © 2008 by Robert Ornstein
ISBN: 978-1-933779-63-8

Library of Congress Cataloging in Publication Data for an earlier hardback edition is as follows:

Library of Congress Catalog card number: 76-149270

"The supreme importance of the problem for all kinds of human values, as well as scientific matters, prompts us to search ahead of the evidence from time to time as science advances for any possible new insight. Even a partial solution that would enable us to decide between very broad and general alternatives — like whether consciousness is cosmic or individual, mortal or immortal, in possession of free will or subject to causal determinism, and the like — could have profound and far-reaching ideological implications."

— Roger Sperry

Contents

Preface to the 2008 edition

I wrote this essay in 1970, when meditation was a curiosity, known only to a few tie-dyed people and, of course, the Beatles. There were spasms of "Transcendental Meditation" burgeoning, a few obscure Zen centers, odd Yogas, and more.

I wanted to see if there was anything to it and, if so, what it told us for human development and our psychology. I found that, all over the world, people had found that similar techniques (you'll have to read the book) yielded similar results. There was method in their method, not madness.

Yogis stare at an object, dervishes repeat a phrase, Zennies concentrate on the inexplicable questions such as "show me your face before your father and mother met."

What are they doing? Recycling the same information through the nervous system, and this has positive effects, if under control and well organized. It provides a respite from ongoing noise of the world and the insides of plans and worries. It is even used in relaxation.

But it also, as I have written here, leads to a different mode of perception.

That's where it was, 38 years ago, and this book now looks like a good basic introduction to the high-tech research that followed (I used mere electroencephalographs). I looked in March 2008 on Google for "meditation" and either "psychology," or "cognition," or "neuroscience." There are 140,000 entries!

Now PET scans reveal changes in the brain during meditation, now corporate Human Resources Managers run meditation classes, it's taught in evening classes, and in high school and even in prisons. The book gives an idea of why.

Robert Ornstein
March 2008

Foreword

This essay is the result of a long process of learning that I didn't really know what I thought I knew. I had studied much of the Western psychological literature on consciousness until I thought I knew. As I began to look elsewhere, to Zen, to Yoga, to the Sufis, I began to understand how little progress we had made in the analysis of the nature of consciousness, and that the richness of the Eastern psychologies had much to offer us. This essay is my attempt to begin to encompass the concepts and techniques of Eastern psychologies in Western terms. What seems to result is a strange mixture of techniques, from computers and electroencephalographs to mantra and dervish dancing.

I have many to thank for different aspects of my education, but I'll mention few. My association with Joe Kamiya allowed and allows me to absorb many of the intricacies of fancy equipment and some of the enthusiasm for physiological feedback. David Galin has been a continuous source of calm yet hysterical and wise advice on many of my vague mumblings — the many times he simply said, "What could you possibly mean by *that?*" Several of the ideas in this manuscript are at least half his.

I am indebted also to Miss Beverly Timmons for her enthusiastic organization of a study group on meditation, as well as for many points of information.

The only previous attempt to consider the practices of meditation within modern psychology has been that of Arthur Deikman. Where his essay touches on similar aspects of meditation, this analysis is similar to, and greatly influenced by, his work. I am in his debt as much for his conceptual analysis as for the demonstration that an attempt to bring meditation within psychology is possible and fruitful.

The interaction with Claudio Naranjo has been fruitful for me in many ways, beyond that of this book. Claudio and I have extremely different backgrounds: he is Chilean, a psychiatrist interested in therapy, psychedelics, etc.; I am an American interested in consciousness and psychophysiology. Early in 1969 we decided that our differences in outlook could produce an interesting book on meditation [this was the original edition, that contains an essay by Naranjo and this one], his part to discuss the experiential aspects and mine to cover the psychology and physiology. We wrote our essays geographically and temporally separated, and we found that the phenomena of the esoteric psychologies seemed to compel similar conclusions. We divided the different types of meditative exercises in basically similar ways: the concentrative form involving a restriction of attention, and an "opening up" form. Naranjo's manuscript, **The Unfolding of Man**, provided me with many new inputs and ideas.

For reading and commenting on earlier versions of the manuscript I am indebted to Enoch Callaway, Charles Tart, Katie Kocel, Charles Furst, Ivan Pasternak, Roger Kramer — and to many others, thank you.

Thanks also to Majo Keleshian, Ann Skillion, and Ruby Collins for typing and retyping the manuscript, and to Faith Hornbacher.

I was supported during the time of writing by a fellowship from the National Institutes of Mental Health, USPHS 2 TI MH 7082-10; by a grant from the Babcock Foundation, with special thanks to Mike Murphy and Barbara Lassiter; and a grant from Janet and Merrill Bickford.

Introduction

When we view the practices of the esoteric disciplines from the vantage point of scientific inquiry, we may put forth ideas and conceptions which to the adherents of the esoteric traditions will be minor or irrelevant. My intention is not to "reduce" totally the phenomena of the esoteric disciplines to psychological terms, but simply to begin the process of considering these aspects of the traditions which fall within the realm of a modern psychological analysis. (Several of the major tenets of these traditions remain outside this form of inquiry.) A similar point has been made by many scientists as well as by those belonging to these traditions. The physicist Robert Oppenheimer has said: "These two ways of thinking, the way of time and history, and the way of eternity and timelessness, are both parts of man's effort to comprehend the world in which he lives. Neither is comprehended in the other nor reducible to it...each supplementing the other, neither telling the whole story."[1]

If we consider a blind man interested in the phenomena of color, there are certain useful operations that he can perform on colored light. He might construct a machine that prints out (in Braille) the wavelength of light.

He might perform certain calculations on his observations, which would enable him, for instance, to predict the wavelength of a new combination of lights, in a wide variety of conditions. We do understand, however, that his analysis in terms of the numbers obtained when a new mixture of lights is combined is in an entirely different order of knowledge from that of the direct experience of color. The Sufi Idries Shah makes the same point in discussing the meaning of the word "Sufi." He notes that many scholars have wondered about the derivation of the name and that there exist various theories — some say the word has no etymology, some identify it with theosophy, some identify it with the Arab garment of wool. Shah says:

> *But acquaintance with Sufis, let alone almost any degree of access to their practices and moral traditions, could easily have resolved any seeming contradiction between the existence of a word and its having no ready etymological derivation. The answer is that the Sufis regard sounds of the letters S, U, F (in Arabic, the signs for soad, wao, fa) as significant in the same order of use in their effect on human mentation.*
>
> *The Sufis are, therefore, the people of SSSSUUUUFFFF.*
>
> *Having disposed of that conundrum (incidentally illustrating the difficulties of getting to grips with Sufi ideas where one thinks only along certain lines), we immediately see a fresh and characteristic problem arising to replace it. The contemporary thinker is likely to be interested in this explanation — this idea that sound influences the brain — only within the limitations imposed by himself. He may accept it as a theoretical possibility insofar as it is expressed in terms that are regarded as admissible at the time of communication.*
>
> *If we say "Sounds have an effect on man, making it possible, other things being equal, for him to have experiences beyond the normal," he may persuasively insist that "This is*

mere occultism, primitive nonsense of the order of OM-MANI-PADME-HUM abracadabra, and the rest." But (taking into account not objectivity, but simply the current phase of accepted thought) we can say to him instead, "The human brain, as you are doubtless aware, may be likened to an electronic computer. It responds to impacts or vibrations of sight, sound, touch, etc., in certain predetermined or 'programmed' ways. It is held by some that the sounds roughly represented by the signs S-U-F are among those for reaction to which the brain is, or may be, 'programmed.'" He may be very well able to assimilate this wretched simplification of the existing pattern of thinking. [2]

We should keep Shah and Oppenheimer's comments in mind, and also remember that portions of this essay may be considered, from the viewpoint of modern psychology, in just the opposite way — as too general and as yet lacking in precise experimental verification, such as which specific brain structures are involved, etc.

This essay, however, is an attempt to begin to prepare a new middle ground between two approaches and to "translate" some of the metaphors of the esoteric traditions into those of modern psychology. The first chapter contains a consideration of the communalities of concentrative meditation exercises with an eye to the common experiences these techniques produce and their possible common effects on the nervous system. This will involve retracing part of Naranjo's path; many of the same techniques and phenomena will be considered from a slightly different viewpoint and move in a slightly different direction. The second chapter is an attempt to point out the essential similarities between the esoteric and modern psychologies of awareness and a consideration of the effects and aftereffects of the practices of meditation on awareness. The third chapter puts forth a "new" view arising within the scientific community of the capabilities of self-regulation of internal states that man possesses, and the aid that modern technology may be in implementing this extended view of our capacity. This "new" view within science is one at least thousands of years old to those of the esoteric traditions.

Chapter One :

"Turning Off" Awareness

A story that appears in Philip Kapleau's **The Three Pillars of Zen** provides us with a useful point at which to begin a psychological consideration of the practices of meditation.

> *The importance of single-mindedness, of bare attention, is illustrated in the following anecdote:*
>
> *One day a man of the people said to the Zen master Ikkyu: "Master, will you please write for me some maxims of the highest wisdom?"*
>
> *Ikkyu immediately took his brush and wrote the word "Attention."*
>
> *"Is that all?" asked the man. "Will you not add something more?"*
>
> *Ikkyu then wrote twice running: "Attention. Attention."*
>
> *"Well," remarked the man rather irritably, "I really don't see much depth or subtlety in what you have just written."*
>
> *Then Ikkyu wrote the same word three times running: "Attention. Attention. Attention."*
>
> *Half-angered, the man demanded: "What does that word, 'Attention' mean anyway?" And Ikkyu answered, gently: "Attention means attention."* [1]

There are many clues in other places that meditation is primarily an exercise in deployment of attention rather than in reason or concept formation. And yet the only major attempt in modern psychology to discuss the practices of meditation, using the concept of attention as the central element of analysis, has been that of Arthur Deikman.

An analysis of any experiential phenomenon in terms of science, in this case in terms of the psychology and physiology of awareness, is naturally more limited, restricted, and drier than actual descriptions of experience. When we try to bring experience within the limiting frame of reference of science, a great deal of the richness and complexity is lost in the attempt to gain a great deal of precision. We will be forced to consider only those points that are amenable to this type of analysis.

Another consideration in this analysis is that most techniques of meditation do not exist as solitary practices but are only artificially separable from an entire system of practice and belief. A given meditation exercise cannot be perfectly understood as an isolated technique but only as an integral part of a whole discipline. The entire process usually, but not always, involves many components, a belief structure, and various forms of concurrent practices. A major component is a detachment from, or even a renunciation of, world activity. Another is a concentration on an energy form called in Yoga *kundalini*. Its activation involves special exercises said to release a form of energy through the spine; this is often combined with special breathing exercises, *pranayama*. Self-observation, which can be considered another form of meditation, is practiced in Zen, Yoga, and Sufism.

Since the general state of our knowledge about the various forms of meditation within science in particular, and within the West in general, is extremely low, we should perhaps first set the background and review some of the general similarities of the meditation exercises. Most involve separating the practitioner from the daily ongoing activities. He usually sits alone or with a small group in a special room set aside for meditation, or in a special place often constructed in a naturally isolated area, a quiet wood, near a waterfall, or a cave. Generally, the attempt is made to keep all external sources of stimulation to a minimum to avoid distracting the meditator from his object of meditation. This isolation is felt to be especially critical in modern cities, where random sounds or human voices can distract the person from his exercise. In most forms of Yoga and in Zen there is emphasis on maintaining a specific posture, the lotus position. This is done for the purpose of keeping bodily movements to a minimum and therefore out of awareness during the meditation period. The stiff back is said, additionally, to lessen the possibility of drowsiness in the reduced stimulation setting. Incense is often burned during meditation to provide a strong consistent background odor to keep out any small distracting changes in smells.

Instructions for most of the meditation exercises are to attend closely and continuously to the meditation object. This is more difficult than it would seem, and most beginners lose awareness of the meditation object quite often. Each time one notices that awareness has shifted from the object of meditation, the instructions are always to return awareness back to the meditation object. In many traditions, each session of meditation lasts about half an hour. In most, although not all, meditation is practiced twice a day, often in the morning before the day's major work, and in the evening. Beginners usually practice for less time and work up to about a half-hour a day, and as progress is made, more and more complicated exercises are usually given.

In terms of the psychology of consciousness, there seem to be two general varieties of meditation: those exercises which involve restriction of awareness, focusing of attention on the object of meditation or the repetition of a word (which Claudio Naranjo terms "concentrative meditation"), and those which involve a deliberate attempt to "open up" awareness of the external environment. We will consider the first form, that of "concentrative" meditation, in this chapter.

In reviewing the extraordinary diversity of the actual techniques of this form of meditation, one general similarity seems to come through. No matter the object of meditation or the superficial practice of meditation, the exercises seem to be attempts to restrict awareness to a single, unchanging source of stimulation for a definite period of time. In many traditions, successfully achieving this is termed "one-pointedness of mind."

If the exercise involves vision, the meditator gazes at the object of meditation continuously. If the meditation is auditory, the sound, the chant, or the prayer is repeated over and over again, either aloud or silently. If the meditation consists in physical movement, the movement is repeated again and again. In all cases, awareness is directed completely on the movement, or the visual object, or the sound.

In Zen, as a first exercise, the student is instructed to count his breaths from one to ten, and on reaching ten to return to one and repeat. When the count is lost, as it will be by beginners, the instructions are that "the count should be returned to one and begun again." After he is able to concentrate completely on his breaths, the student then begins a more advanced exercise and focuses attention on the *process* of breathing itself. He thinks about nothing but the movement of the air within himself, the air reaching his nose, going down into the lungs, remaining in the lungs, and finally the process of exhalation. This is a convenient way to begin meditation, since breathing is a natural activity, which continues whether we will it or not. This is not an attempt to control the normal breathing as in some aspects of the Yoga and Sufi traditions, but simply to be aware of the breathing and to maintain this awareness on the breathing and nothing else.

In ***What the Buddha Taught,*** Walpola Rahula gives these instructions:

> *You breathe in and out all day and night, but you are never mindful of it, you never for a second concentrate your mind on it. Now you are going to do just this. Breathe in and out as usual, without any effort or strain. Now, bring your mind to concentrate on your breathing-in and breathing-out, let your mind watch and observe your breathing in and out; let your mind be aware and vigilant of your breathing in and out. When you breathe, you sometimes take deep breaths, sometimes not. This does not matter at all. Breathe normally and naturally. The only thing is that when you take deep breaths you should be aware that they are deep breaths, and so on. In other words, your mind should be so fully concentrated on your breathing that you are aware of its movements and changes. Forget all other things, your surroundings, your environment; do not raise your eyes and look at anything. Try to do this for five or ten minutes.*

> *At the beginning you will find it extremely difficult to bring your mind to concentrate on your breathing. You will be astonished how your mind runs away. It does not stay. You begin to think of various things. You hear sounds outside. Your mind is disturbed and distracted. You may be dismayed and disappointed. But if you continue to practice this exercise twice a day, morning and evening, for about five or ten minutes at a*

time, you will gradually, by and by, begin to concentrate your mind on your breathing. After a certain period you will experience just that split second when your mind is fully concentrated on your breathing, when you will not hear even sounds nearby, when no external world exists for you. This slight moment is such a tremendous experience for you, full of joy, happiness and tranquility, that you would like to continue it. But still you cannot. Yet, if you go on practicing this regularly, you may repeat the experience again and again for longer and longer periods. That is the moment, when you lose yourself completely in your mindfulness of breathing. As long as you are conscious of yourself you cannot concentrate on anything. ²

As the student of Rinzai Zen progresses, he learns to keep himself motionless, to sit in the quite difficult lotus position, and as he learns to maintain awareness of his breath successfully, he is given a more advanced meditation exercise.

A riddle or paradox, called a *koan*, is given him to meditate upon. To most commentators the koan has been the subject of much misunderstanding and confusion. The question-and-answer routine has seemed to be one for the Marx Brothers. The "question" may be, "Show me your face before your mother and father met." The "answer" may be the student slapping the questioner in the face. The master asks the student, "Move that boat on the lake right now with your mind!," and the student stands up, runs over and hits his head against the gong, turns a somersault, and lands in front of the master. Since the student answered successfully, it is quite clear that the "answers" to the koan are not to be considered logically in the sense of their being rational problems with set answers, to be solved in the usual manner of thinking through various rational alternatives and choosing one.

We might instead consider the koan exercise in the more restricted terms of the psychology of awareness. In these terms, the koan is an extreme and compelling method of forcing intense concentration one single thought. The first koan exercise is:

> *In all seriousness a monk asked Joshu, "Has the dog Buddha nature or not?"*
> *Joshu retorted, "Mu!"**

This koan is not to be taken verbally and logically, to be worked through like a problem, but as an extreme exercise in concentration. This is confirmed in instructions given in the lectures of a contemporary Zen master, Yasutani Roshi;

> *You must concentrate day and night, questioning yourself about* Mu *through every one of your 360 bones and 84,000 pores . . . what this refers to is your entire being. Let all of you become one mass of doubt and questioning. Concentrate on and penetrate fully into* Mu. *To penetrate into* Mu *is to achieve this unity by holding to* Mu *tenaciously day and night! Do not separate yourself from it under any circumstances! Focus your mind on it constantly. Do not construe* Mu *as nothingness and do not conceive it in terms of existence or non-existence. You must not, in other words, think of* Mu *as a problem involving the existence or non-existence of Buddha-nature. Then what do you do? You stop speculating and concentrate wholly on* Mu *—just* Mu! [3]

Later koan exercises involve other unanswerable questions, such as "What is the sound of one hand clapping?" and "What is the size of the real you?"

---

*Mu *is a word that has no meaning in Japanese.*

Because no verbal logical answer to the question can be found, the koan becomes a useful and demanding focus of attention over a very long period of time. The koan becomes a meditation object, day and night, a constant and compelling focusing of awareness on a single source. The lack of a rational, logical solution forces the student to go through and to discard all his verbal associations, all his thoughts, all his "solutions" — the conceptual processing usually evoked by a question. He is then forced by the nature of the question to approach the condition known as "one-pointedness" — concentrating solely on one thing: the "unanswerable" koan.

Focusing attention is helped by the demands put on the student, by the pressures he imposes upon himself to achieve a breakthrough (to solve the koan), by the attitude of his fellow students, and by his interviews (*dokusan*) with the Zen master, the *roshi*. In the interviews the Zen student is often asked to demonstrate his level of understanding by giving an answer to the koan. Obviously, the desired answer is not verbal or logical; ideally it should be a communication of a new level of awareness brought about by the process of concentrating on the koan. The "correct" answer, which may be one of many possible ones, seems strange only on a logical level; it is intended to communicate on a different level. The koan is perhaps one of the most extreme techniques to delimit awareness.

The use of the koan is strongest in the Rinzai school of Zen, which places emphasis on sudden alterations of awareness brought about by this extreme concentration on one point over a long period of time under stress. The Soto school of Zen emphasizes another technique involving a different type of meditation exercise.

This second technique is termed "just sitting" (*shikan-taza*) and is an example of the form of meditation in which a deliberate attempt is made to open up awareness of the external environment. The Soto method emphasizes a much more gradual development than does the Rinzai sect, which places the emphasis on sudden flashes of expanded awareness as the aftereffect of the koan exercise. The second form of meditation, that of opening up awareness while meditating, will be considered at greater length again in the next chapter.

The practices of Yoga are much more varied than those of Zen. Concentrative meditation in Yoga is only a part of the totality of activity, and each part is considered a contributing factor to alterations of consciousness. Many Yoga practitioners devote much of their time to attempts to alter basic "involuntary" physiological processes -- blood flow, heart rate, digestive activity, muscular activity, breathing, etc. There are various reports of Yoga masters being buried alive for long periods of time, of stopping their blood flow, of walking barefoot on hot coals, etc. Anand and his associates have found that some yogis can reduce oxygen consumption to levels far below that of normal.[4]

A major component of Yoga involves training in breath control (*pranayama*). Different cycles of breathing are used and different depths of breathing are practiced, in order to obtain some alterations (presumably) in blood oxygen content, carbon dioxide, etc., and the resulting changes in awareness. In these attempts at altering physiological processes, Yoga differs from Zen, where there is no attempt to control breathing or heart activity. The one Zen meditation exercise that does involve breathing is one in which the student simply observes his breathing, as it occurs, rather than attempting in any way to control it. Many of the meditation exercises in Yoga are, however, quite similar to Zen.

A common form of yogic meditation practice involves the use of mantra. Mantra are often words of significance, names of the deity, but in terms of the psychology of consciousness the important element is that the technique uses a word as the focus of awareness, just as the first Zen exercises make use of breathing. The instructions are to repeat the mantram over and over again, either aloud or silently. The mantram is to be kept in awareness to the exclusion of all else. This is similar to the first Zen exercise, in that when awareness lapses from the breathing, the attention is to be returned to it. Mantra are sonorous, mellifluous words, which repeat easily. An example is OM. This mantram is chanted aloud in groups, or used individually in silent or voiced meditation. Another is OM-MANI-PADME-HUM, a smooth mellifluous chant. Similar mantra have analogous sounds such as AYN, HUM, etc., somewhat similar in sound to *Mu* in the first Zen koan. All include sonorous consonants — M's, H's, any many vowels.

Another well-known mantram is the Hare Krishna mantram. This is always chanted aloud in a group. The mantram itself involves a lot of repetition, and the entire mantram is repeated over and over.

HARE KRISHNA
HARE KRISHNA
KRISHNA KRISHNA
HARE HARE
HARE RAMA
HARE RAMA
RAMA RAMA
HARE HARE

A form of Mantram Yoga, "Transcendental Meditation," has become fairly well known in the West, especially in the United States. In this form of meditation, too, the practitioner is given a specific mantram and he is to repeat it silently over and over for about a half-hour twice a day, in the morning and in the evening. No special posture is required for the exercise; rather one is instructed to assume a comfortable posture, such as sitting erect in a chair. The thoughts that arise during the meditation are considered to be of no significance, and as soon as one is aware that one is no longer focused on the mantram, attention is to be returned to it.

The specific mantra used in "Transcendental Meditation" are not given publicly, since the devotees of this technique claim that there are special effects of each one in addition to the general effects of concentration. But it can be noted here that these mantra are also mellifluous and smooth, including many M's, Y's and vowels, similar to OM or MU in Zen. The devotees of "Transcendental Meditation" also claim that this technique involves the essence of meditation in a form suitable for Western persons. There is no doubt that Mantram Yoga, including "Transcendental Meditation," is a very convenient form of meditation. As in the breathing exercises, it is quite easy to produce and attend to a silent word, anywhere, at any time. Since there is no special posture required, the arduous training for sitting in a lotus position is unnecessary. If the essential component of meditation involves concentration on an unchanging stimulus, then "Transcendental Meditation," as well as other forms of Mantram Yoga, can be said to possess this essence.

Other forms of Yoga practice make use of visual meditation techniques. The yogin generally sits in a lotus position and views a specially constructed visual image, a mandala. Mandalas take many forms: they may be very simple, like a circle, or extremely complicated, as in the yantra of Tantra practice.

Mandalas are used similarly to mantra. The practitioner focuses his gaze on the mandala and restricts his awareness to the visual input. Any stray thought or association or feeling that arises is suppressed, and awareness is returned from the stray thought or association back to the mandala. Simple mandalas often employ a circular motif in which awareness is drawn to the center, as one continues to contemplate, fixing one's gaze more and more closely on the center.

Another visual meditation technique in Yoga involves a "steady gaze" (*tratakam*) on external objects. External objects are used in meditation to provide a focus for a fixed point of concentration, rather than for their teacher of the particular sect of Yoga, but it can be a stone, a vase, a light, a candle, etc. Rammamurti Mishra, in his manual **Fundamentals of Yoga,** gives instructions for some of these practices.

> *1. Exterior surface of the body*
>
> *a. Nasal gaze: Keep your eyes half closed, half open, and steadily gaze at the tip of the nose. Practice regularly in the morning and in the evening; when the eyes are tired or tearing, close them fully and meditate one minute fully in that state....*
>
> *b.* Buru madhya dristi *(frontal gaze): Fix your power of attention at the center between the eyebrows, turn your half-closed eyes towards the space between the eyebrows; like the nasal gaze, the frontal gaze is a powerful exercise to control wandering thoughts and mind....*
>
> *c.* Tratakam *on external objects: Select a picture of a perfect yogi or respected teacher, or you can select some small round object on the wall of your room if you do not know any liberated*

soul: a round object, a miniature, a small round point, or zero. Think of the thing selected, that is, the symbolic nature, and by gazing at the symbol you are gazing at supreme consciousness and supreme nature. Fix yourself in such a posture and position so that you may see this object easily, neither too far from it nor too near to it. Look at this object steadily, practice constantly and regularly, never gaze long enough to tire your eyes, close your eyes and meditate when your feel strained. After a few months of constant and regular practice, you will increase your power to stare at this object almost indefinitely without strain, fatigue and blinking....

d. Tratakam *on blue light: Place a bed lamp with a blue, very low voltage bulb at the head of your bed or other suitable place so that you can gaze easily; now light the lamp and recline on the bed or in an easy chair in the most comfortable posture.... Now gaze directly at the bulb in such a way that you do not blink your eyes but the bulb is directly overhead and you are peering intently at it; your gaze must be steady and continuous and constant; concentrate fully on the bulb....*[5]

The repetitive processes of the body, such as breathing and heart beats, can serve as similar foci for concentration in Yoga. These techniques are described in Mishra's manual and in many others.

Internally generated sounds (*nadam*) can similarly serve as the focus of meditation. Mishra gives some examples, of which the following are the most useful and frequent.

CIN NADAM: Like the hum of the honey of intoxicated bees; idling engine vibration; rainfall, whistling sounds, high frequency sounds
CIN CIN NADAM: waterfall, roaring of an ocean
GHANTA NADAM: sound of a bell ringing
SANKHA NADAM: sound of a conch shell

TANTRI VINA: nasal sound, humming sound like that
of a wire string instrument
TELA NADAM: sound of a small, tight drum
VENA NADAM: sound of a flute
MRIDAMGA NADAM: sound of a big brass drum
BHERI NADAM: echoing sound
MEGA NADAM: roll of distant thunder [6]

The sounds used in meditation can be either imagined
or naturally occurring. Often the yogin sits near a natural
source of repetitive sound, such as a waterfall, wind source,
humming of bees, and simply listens and concentrates.
When these repetitious, monotonous sounds are imagined,
the technique becomes quite similar to the silent repetition
of a mantram.

Creation of a meditation image can extend to visual
types of meditation as well. Frederick Spiegelberg, in
Spiritual Practices of India, describes the *dharana,*
or fixation of consciousness procedures — the "kasina
exercises":

*The point of primary importance is that one should really
create such a meditation-image to accompany him continuously;
only as a secondary consideration does it matter what this
particular image may be, that is, through which one of the
kasina exercises it has been produced. Instead of contemplating
a disc of earth, for example, one can meditate on an evenly
ploughed field seen from a distance. In the Water Kasina, the
yogi concentrates either on the circular surface of water in a
jar, or on a lake seen from a mountain. So, too, the fire on the
hearth, the flame of a candle, the wind that sways the crests
of the trees may also be used as Kasina. The exercise of Color
Kasina makes use of round colored discs, and even of bright-*

colored flags and flowers. In Space Kasina one meditates on a circular window opening, the attention in this case being directed primarily to the dimensional proportions of the opening.

Every image that remains permanently in one's consciousness and every enduring mood can be a help to this fixation of one's consciousness. As a matter of fact, every hallucination, every unappeasable hatred, every amorous attachment provides a certain power of concentration to him who cherishes it, and helps him direct the forces of his being toward a single goal. This is of course more the case with the man who has achieved self-control and freedom from his passions, and who after having mastered his sense impulses succeeds in giving to his consciousness a definite turn of his own choosing. . . . Every activity is of equal value as a basis for a dharana exercise. [7]

The process of active construction of an image of meditation, in this particular case visual images, is elaborated in Tantra practice. In meditating on the yantra, the image is *created* piece by piece until the yogin can produce it in consciousness at will. Many of the yantras that have been drawn out on paper from memory can be found in Mookerjee's quite beautiful book **Tantra Art.** [8] This type of active visualization also forms a portion of Tibetan Yoga practice. The practices of creating a meditation image have obvious advantages — one need not be present in any special place for meditation and one can reproduce any form at any time — so that many forms of meditation, like breathing and the verbal forms, can be done independently of the circumstance or the place.

Another variety of yogic meditation practice, mudra, involves repetitive physical movements, usually of the arms, legs, and fingers. In these exercises (which are somewhat more difficult to write about since no picture or word is involved) the movement of the limbs is performed and repeated over and over in the same way as mantram. Awareness is continually directed toward the process of making the movements. Mudras vary in complexity; a simple one may involve touching the thumb to the other four fingers in order and repeating this procedure. The mudra may be combined with the mantram. For instance, the above fourfold repetitive mudra could be combined with the mantram OM-MANI-PADME-HUM, each word corresponding to the thumb's movement to a finger.

The Sufis make similar use of repetitive movements. Manuals for Sufic practice do not exist in any readily available form as they do for Yoga and Zen. The Sufis hold that the techniques must be administered, and the time, place and state of the student must be taken into account. Publication of the details of their practice would lead to faulty applications of the exercises. A technique such as meditation, for instance, is held to be useful only at a specific stage of development, and persistence in any technique after the appropriate period might be a waste of time or even harmful.

There are, however, fragmentary reports available of some of the Sufi meditation exercises, which can be summarized here. The Mevlevi (whirling dervishes) are perhaps the best known in the West. They perform a dance involving spinning and repetition of phrases. George Gurdjieff, who was trained by dervishes, explains the dance of the dervishes as an exercise for the brain based on repetition. Idries Shah writes of these orders: "The so-called dancing dervishes accomplish trance and ecstatic phenomena through monotonous repetition circumambulations, and this is marked in the Maulavi order, most popular in Turkey."

The dance of the dervishes involves both the repetition of physical movements and the concurrent repetition of sounds. One of the few available first-person descriptions of this dance is found in Roy Weaver Davidson's valuable symposium, **Documents on Contemporary Dervish Communities**. It is an account by Omar Michael Burke who traveled to a Dervish assembly in Tunisia, and participated in a dervish dance.

Explanation of the Zikr (repetition). *The Dhikr, it was explained to me, is a dance; or, more properly, a performance of a series of exercises in unison. The objective is to produce a state of ritual ecstasy and to accelerate the contact of the Sufi's mind with the world mind, of which he considers himself to be a part...All dervishes and not only the followers of Maulana Rumi (as most Orientalists believe) perform a dance. The dance is defined by them as bodily movements linked to a thought and a sound or a series of sounds. The movements develop the body; the thought focuses the mind and the sound fuses the two and orientates them towards a consciousness of divine contact, which is called* Hal, *meaning "state" or "condition."*

Description of the Zikr at Nefta. *A double circle is formed in the center of the hall. Dervishes stand while the Sheik intones the opening part of this and every similar ceremony — the calling down of the blessing upon the congregation and from the congregation upon the Masters, "past, present and future." Outside the circle stand the Sheik, drummer and flute player, together with two "callers," men who call the rhythm of the dance. The drum begins to beat, the caller begins to call a high-pitched flamenco-type air, and slowly the concentric circles begin to revolve in opposite directions. Then the sheik calls out, "Ya Haadi!" (O Guide!) and the participants start to repeat this word. They concentrate on it, saying it at first slowly, then faster and faster. Their movements match the repetitions.*

I noticed that the eyes of some of the dervishes took on a far-away look and they started to move jerkily as if they were puppets. The circles moved faster and faster until I (moving in the outer circle) saw only a whirl of robes and lost count of time. Now and then, with a grunt or a sharp cry, one of the dervishes would drop out of the circle and would be led away by an assistant, to lie on the ground in what seemed to be an hypnotic state. I began to be affected and found that, although I was not dizzy, my mind was functioning in a very strange and unfamiliar way. The sensation is difficult to describe and is probably a complex one. One feeling was that of a lightening; as if I had no anxieties, no problems. Another was that I was a part of this moving circle and that my individuality was gone, I was delightfully merged in something larger.

[He leaves the dance, and later] I went out into the courtyard to assess my feelings; something had *happened. In the first place, the moon seemed immensely bright, and the little glowing lamps seemed surrounded by a whole spectrum of colors.* [10]

The Sufis use other forms of concentrative meditation, some of which, in some aspects, appear quite similar to those of Zen and Yoga. Dhikrs are verbal repetition exercises. The first line of the **Koran** is quite often used for this purpose. Idries Shah thus describes the exercises:

Having either been given a set of Dhikrs to repeat (if he is under the direct guidance of a sheik) or having selected one himself if he is a uwaysi, working towards the goal alone, his task is to repeat it meticulously with regard for the times and frequency of its saying. If the formula is said under the breath, Dhikr Kafi, a rosary with ninety-nine beads, is used, one bead being told after each repetition; in the case of the Dhikr Jali, loud repetition, the rosary is often not used; ...attending an actual Halka circle (meeting) the seeker goes to some quiet place or spends his contemplation time in a room set aside for the purpose.

There is, too, the exercise known as Fikr, which consists of meditation, concentration on some power that is desired or upon the immensity of the universe. When Dhikr and Fikr have been indulged in to such an extent that they become second nature, the superior form of Dhikr becomes necessary. This is the control and concentration of breath. The mind is concentrated upon a single idea, and the original Dhikr form or another is recited, this time in set rhythm corresponding to the breathing. [11]

There exist fragmentary descriptions of other exercises used by the Sufis and some of their followers. A student of George Gurdjieff writes of meditating on a series of dots on a piece of paper.[12] The dervishes repeat the phrase "Ya hud" in a way similar to the Yoga mantra and the Zen koan *Mu*, and also repeat stories over and over in their minds, as Zen Buddhists do with the koan.[13]

In conventional religions more familiar to us in the West, as well as in sects less known than Yoga, Zen, and Sufism, similar kinds of meditation practices exist. In early Christianity, for example, the exercise of contemplation performed a function similar to that of meditation in Zen, Yoga, and Sufism. Jakob Bohme, the Christian mystic, practiced fixing his gaze on a spot of sunlight on his cobbler's crystal as his object of contemplation throughout the entire day. He contemplated sunlight so much that this spot of light remained on his eyes permanently, burning part of the retina. He was then able to carry this image with him all the time, in the same way, perhaps, that the yogi can construct a yantra at will and observe it. Deikman has commented that the Christian mystics Walter Hilton and St. John of the Cross gave instructions for contemplation exercises that were strikingly similar to those of Patanjali, the author of the Yoga sutras.

> *In Hilton one reads, "Therefore if you desire to discover your soul, withdraw your thoughts from outward and material things, forgetting, if possible, your own body and its five senses." St. John calls for the explicit banishment of memory. "Of all these forms and manners of knowledge the soul must strip and void itself and it must strive to lose the imaginary apprehensions of them, so that there may be left in it no kind of impression of knowledge, nor trace of thought whatsoever, but rather the soul must remain barren and bare, as if these forms has never passed through it, and in total oblivion and suspension. This cannot happen unless the memory can be annihilated of all its forms, if it is to be united with God...." Patanjali comments, "Binding the mind stuff to a place is fixed attention, focusing the presented idea on that place is contemplation. This same contemplation shining forth on concentration....The three in one are constraint....even these [three] are indirect aids to seedless [concentration]." [14]*

Some of the current practices in the Christian Church and in Judaism have some similarities and even perhaps their origins in the practices of meditation. Prayer, in general, is a practice most similar to concentrative meditation. St. John Climacus said: "If many words are used in prayer, all sorts of distracting pictures hover in the mind but worship is lost. If little is said or only a single word pronounced, the mind remains concentrated." The "Russian Pilgrim" said: "If thou wilt that thy prayer be pure, made up of good and lovely things, thou must choose a short one consisting of a few powerful words and repeat it many times." Many of the prayers are monotonous, repetitive chants. Judaism makes use also of ritual nodding movements and intoned prayers. Hasidism and Cabalistic tradition contain many elements similar to Zen, Yoga, and Sufism. The cross and the Star of David appear as contemplation objects in traditions other than the Jewish and Christian; some of the yantras in **Tantra Art**, for instance, contain many six-pointed stars. Perhaps one reason for a decline of interest in these more organized religions is that the stress on altering awareness has largely been muted. And, although the techniques for altering awareness still persist, the practices have become "automatic," part of a set ritual, lacking their original purpose.

The Prayer of the Heart in Greek Orthodox tradition, however, is much less removed from the meditative traditions considered. A similar focusing of awareness is also part of Taoist meditation. Instructions are given to sit quietly and focus awareness of the center of the body, on one point, on the abdomen. The medieval alchemists describe long and repetitive exercises — the constant redistillation of water, the prolonged grinding exercises — which were written down allegedly for the "distillation" of base metal for its transmutation into gold. These instructions can also be taken metaphorically as descriptions of attempts to alter man's awareness from his ordinary "base" level to a higher one, symbolized by the gold.[14]

Peter Freuchen, in his **Book of the Eskimos**, describes a technique for meditation in which the Eskimo sits facing a large soft stone; he takes a small hard stone and begins to carve a circle in the larger one by moving the small stone continuously around and around the larger surface. This practice, similar to the creation of a mandala, often lasts for several days at a time and is designed to produce a trance state. Many primitive peoples, such as the Bushmen of the Kalahari Desert, dance in a circle facing a fire, staring at the fire, and repetitiously chanting. Some gaze continuously at the full moon, the sun, or at a candle.

This has been a fairly quick, selective review of some of the major forms of concentrative meditation. Each of the major traditions — Zen, Yoga, and Sufism — has exercises involving the different sensory modalities. A chant is repeated in each of the traditions; a word, koan, mantram, or dervish call is repeated; concentration is focused on the breath, on the heart beat, on the short prayer, longer prayer, story, or on natural sounds, such as a waterfall, or on some imagined sounds, such as the humming of bees, or on vibration. Symbols or pictures of gurus are subjected to steady gaze, and images are created only in the mind's eye of the practitioner, more like imagined sounds silently repeated. Sufi dervishes dance in a repetitive whirl; Indian yogis make continuous movements with their limbs; Taoists concentrate on the abdomen. The early Christian Fathers contemplated an object or the cross. These are all extremely different forms of the same type of meditation.

The strong common element seems to lie in the actual restriction of awareness to one single, unchanging process. It does not seem to matter which actual physical practice is followed; whether one symbol or another is employed; whether the visual system is used or body movements repeated; whether awareness is focused on a limb or on a sound or on a word or on a prayer. This process might be considered in psychological terms as an attempt to recycle the same subroutine over and over again in the nervous system. The instructions for meditation are consistent with this; one is instructed always to rid awareness of any thought save the object of meditation, to shut oneself off from the main flow of ongoing external activity and attend only to the object or process of meditation. Almost any process or object seems usable and has probably been used. The specific object of meditation (for this analysis) is much less important than maintaining the object as the single focus of awareness over a long period of time.

Shah points out that some Tibetans repeat the OM-MANI-PADME-HUM mantra exactly backward, and the following Sufi story from his *Tales of the Dervishes: Teaching-Stories of the Sufi Masters over the Past Thousand Years* illustrates this same point:

> *A conventionally-minded dervish, walking along the shore of a lake, heard another dervish give the dervish call incorrectly. Considering it a duty to correct the unfortunate person who was mispronouncing the syllables, for this was probably someone who had had no guidance and was doing his best to attune himself to the idea behind the sound, he hired a boat and traveled to the island from where the loud shout came. He corrected the other dervish, who thanked him, and he returned to the mainland, feeling satisfied with his own good deed. After all, it is said that a man who could repeat sacred formulas correctly could even walk on the waves.*
>
> *While he was thinking like this, he suddenly saw a strange sight. From the island the other dervish was coming toward him, walking on the surface of the water. "Brother," the dervish said when he was close enough, "I am sorry to trouble you but I had to come out to ask you again the standard method of making the repetition you were telling me, because I find it difficult to remember it."* [15]

The same point is made by a Russian story of three holy men (*staretzi*) who lived in complete isolation on a small island in the Arctic Sea:

> *A bishop heard of them and decided to pay them a visit. On the shore of the island he found three bearded, toothless old men who bowed low before him. The bishop asked how they prayed. The old man replied: "We pray thus: 'Ye are three; we*

are three; have mercy on us!' The bishop was amazed at this and began to teach them how to pray. He taught them the Lord's Prayer until they knew it by heart. They thanked him fervently for the lesson. Then he went aboard his ship with a glad heart for performing a good deed. His ship had been sailing for a while when strange clouds formed on the horizon, and quickly approached. Suddenly the passengers realized that the clouds were the forms of three men. The three men bowed low before the bishop and told him sadly that they had forgotten the newly learnt prayer. Would he have the graciousness and patience to teach it to them again. Then the bishop crossed himself, bowed to the staretzi and said: "God will hear your prayer as it is. There is nothing I can teach you. Go and pray for us sinners." The bishop prostrated himself before them. But they turned around and went over the water back to the island. And until the dawn, a light streamed forth, at the place where the pious staretzi had vanished.[16]

It seems that the mode of meditation, too, makes little difference. The primary effect can be considered as a central state evoked by the process of repetition. The stress on the communality of the techniques of meditation need not necessarily conflict with the contention of those of the esoteric traditions that certain forms of meditation may have *additional* specific effects on specific individuals. The Maharishi Mahesh Yogi, the originator of the "Transcendental Meditation" movement, feels that a specific mantram must be given to each individual. Shah "wretchedly simplifies" for Western observers and states that the letters S, U, F in Arab pronunciation have a *specific* effect on consciousness. At a level beyond that of this analysis, the Sufis also hold that specific tales can communicate knowledge in dimensions other than the ordinary.[17]

But, since the general level of knowledge within science about the actual practices of meditation is so scanty, the stress here is on the *major communality* of the techniques of concentrative meditation across disciplines, across sensory modalities.

These techniques are said in the traditions to lead to a "one-pointedness" or to a "clear" state of awareness. The state is generally described as "dark," or in Indian terminology, "the void," or "emptiness." It is a withdrawal of the senses, a "turning off" of perception of the external world. In yogic practice this withdrawal is most explicitly sought. In Buddhist meditation the stress is more often on an expanded rather that restricted awareness. But recall that Rahula says, in describing the breathing meditation, that "after a certain period you will have experienced just that split second when your mind is fully concentrated on your breathing, when you will not hear even sounds nearby, when no external world exists for you."* Augustine Poulain describes it as "a mysterious darkness wherein is contained the limitless Good, a void, other than solitude." St. John describes it as the "annihilation of memory."

It may be that men in different places at different times have noticed that by repeating an action or a phrase over and over again, or continuously focusing on breathing, the awareness of the external world can be shut out. Since we, the Bushmen, the Eskimos, the monks of Tibet, the Zen masters, the Yoga adepts, and the dervishes all share a common nervous system, it is not so surprising that similarities in techniques should have evolved.

These techniques have persisted for centuries. Many sensory modalities have been employed, and many different symbols or objects within any one sensory modality have been used. This may indicate that one primary effect

---

* *See page 9.*

of the concentrative meditation exercises is the state of emptiness, the non-response to the external world, evoked in the central nervous system by the continuous subroutine called up by the exercise regardless of the specific nature of the input or the sensory modality employed.

There is a whole body of work on the psychological and physiological effects of restricting awareness to an unchanging stimulus. One variety of concentrative meditation discussed involves a "steady gaze" on either a natural object or a specially constructed one, a "mandala." A very similar situation would arise if input to the eye were always the same, no matter how one moved one's eyes.

Normally, as we look at the world, our eyes move around and fixate at various points in large movements called "saccades." We hardly ever gaze steadily at any one object for a prolonged period of time. Even when we try to fix our vision on a single object, very small involuntary movements of the eye occur, called "optical nystagmus." The image on the retina is kept in constant motion by both these types of eye movements.

A group of physiological psychologists succeeded in devising a system that enables a visual image to remain constant on the retina even though the eyes are in constant motion. One apparatus for producing this "stabilized" image consists of an extremely small projector mounted on a contact lens worn by the subject. The contact lens moves with every movement of the eyeball, and no matter how the eye is moved, the same image falls on the retina.[18] *(See Figure 1.)*

This study of stabilized images was undertaken in psychology primarily to investigate a theory of Donald Hebb, according to which continuously varied input is needed to maintain normal awareness. It was felt that "stabilizing" the image would eliminate the continuous

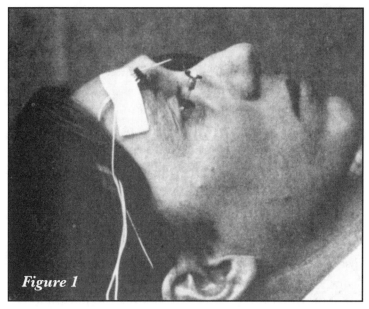

Figure 1

changes in input that normally occur as we move our eyes in space.

The effect on awareness of stabilizing the visual image is consistent: the image tends to disappear completely. The fact that it does tend to reappear periodically in some studies is most likely due to the slipping of the contact lens on the eyes. When an image is stabilized on the retina with extreme precision, using the internal structure of the eye as the stimulus, the image disappears in a few seconds and never returns.

Lehmann, Beeler, and Fender attempted to investigate the brain state evoked by the stabilized image.[19] The electroencephalogram (EEG) as recorded at the scalp, consists of the tiny electrical potentials that emanate from the brain. These tiny potentials, about 5 - 50-millionths of a volt, are amplified and written out on paper by the electroencephalograph. The first brain rhythm was discovered by Berger in 1924, and termed the "alpha" rhythm, which consists of rhythmic activity between 8 and 12 Hz. Since Berger, other rhythms have been classified: beta, defined as 12 cycles and above, theta, 4 - 7; and delta, 1 - 4. The alpha rhythm is usually thought of as representing a state of decreased visual attention to the external environment. It is increased almost always when the eyes are closed or when the eyes are rolled up into the head — when vision is turned down.

Lehmann, Beeler, and Fender recorded the EEG from the occipital cortex of the brain while their subject was viewing the stabilized image. They asked their subject to press a button when the stabilized image disappeared, and attempted to correlate the subjective experience of the disappearance of the image with the concurrent brain state. They found that the alpha rhythm was likely to appear at the time when the subject reported the disappearance of the image. Alpha rhythm, in this case too, seems associated with a decrease in awareness of the external world.

Another means of supplying consistent visual input provides the observer with a completely patternless visual field, called a "ganzfeld." This field can be produced in many ways. A whitewashed surface can serve as a ganzfeld. Cohen, in a series of studies, produced his ganzfeld using two spheres, each 1 meter in diameter.[20] Hochberg, Triebel, and Seaman produced a homogeneous visual field more conveniently by taping halved ping-pong balls over the observer's eyes.[21] The effect on consciousness of the ganzfeld situation is similar to that of the stabilized image.

Cohen found that some observers reported an absence of any visual experience — what they called "blank out." This was not merely the experience of seeing nothing, but that of *not seeing*, a complete disappearance of the sense of vision for short periods of time, as Cohen puts it. The feeling of not seeing at all usually occurred after about twenty minutes of exposure to the ganzfeld. During blank-out the observers did not know, for instance, whether their eyes were open or not, and they could not even control their eye movements. Cohen's suggestion was that this continuous uniform stimulation resulted in the failure of any kind of image to be produced in consciousness. He also found that the periods of blank-out were associated with bursts of alpha rhythm. He suggested that the appearance of alpha during these continuous stimulation periods indicated a functional similarity between continuous stimulation and no stimulation at all. He also found that individuals with high alpha EEG's were more susceptible to the blank-out phenomenon.

Tepas performed a study on the ganzfeld similar to that of Lehmann, Beeler, and Fender's on the stabilized image.[22] His observers watched the ganzfeld for five-minute periods while EEG's were recorded. When the observer experienced the blank-out, he was asked to press a microswitch that marked the EEG record. Tepas found that the alpha activity of the brain was increased during the period of blank-out.

Both the stabilized image and the ganzfeld situation are very similar to the practices of concentrative meditation. Consider the activity of the observer in meditation and in the two precisely regulated input situations: in both an attempt is made to provide unchanging input. Analogous is the subjective experience in both situations: a loss of contact with the external world. In all these conditions the state of the brain indicates an increase in alpha rhythm. The electrophysiological studies of meditation by Bagchi and Wanger,[23] those by Anand and others in India on Yoga meditation,[24] and those by Kasamatsu and Hirai,[25] and by Akishige in Japan on Zen meditation[26] indicate that meditation also is a high alpha state. The more precisely controlled situations seem to produce, both psychologically and physiologically, effects similar to those of concentrative meditation.

The stabilized image and ganzfeld condition in themselves indicate that the phenomenon or blank-out, or disappearance of the stabilized image, or loss of contact with the external world, is due to effects on the central nervous system rather than on the characteristics of the peripheral senses. The effects of stabilized images are transferred between the eyes, indicating that the disappearance phenomenon must occur somewhere later in the visual system than in the retina. Stimulation in other sensory modalities (the sudden onset of a noise, for example) also returns the stabilized image back into consciousness.

It seems that a consequence of the structure of our central nervous system is that if awareness is restricted to one unchanging source of stimulation, a "turning off" of consciousness of the external world follows. Common instructions for meditation all underscore this; one is continually advised to be aware of the object of meditation and nothing else, to continuously recycle the same input over and over. Stabilizing a visual image or homogenizing visual input results in the same experience. A set of instructions by Knowles of the English mystical tradition indicates that this blanking-out is a desired function of meditation that can be produced by restriction of awareness.

> *Forget all creatures that God ever made, and the works of them so that thy thought or thy desire be not directed or stretched to any of them, neither in general nor in special...At the first time when thou dost it thou findest but a darkness and as it were a kind of unknowing, thou knowest not what, saving that thou feelest in thy will a naked intent unto God.*[27]

The interpretations of this experience of "darkness," of "blank-out," of the "void," of the disappearance of an image in the subject of a scientific experiment, would certainly differ: the subject of a physiological experiment would have extremely different expectations and ideas about his experience than a man who has sought this experience as part of his meditative practice. But the experiences themselves have essential similarities and are produced simply and through quite similar procedures.

So the practices of meditation — whirling, chanting, concentrating on a nonsensical question, repeating a prayer over and over again, picturing a cross, looking at a vase, counting breaths, etc. — are probably not quite so exotic as those who seek the exotic and esoteric would like, and are not properly considered as exercises in reasoning or problem-solving,[28] but rather as exercises in restriction of attention. The somewhat bewildering superficial differences in the various practices — the koan, the mantram, the mudra, the mandala, the kasina exercises, the dharana exercises, the dhikr, the fhikr, the dance of the Mevlevi dervishes, the Taoist meditation on the abdomen, the "Prayer of the Heart:" — all can be understood as aids in focusing awareness of a single process, continuously recycling the same subroutine through the nervous system. When this is achieved, a common experience seems to be produced: awareness of the external environment diminishes and "turns off" for a period of time.

Psychologically, continuous repetition of the same stimulus may be considered the equivalent of no stimulation at all. The two situations, which from the psychological and physiological points of view are quite similar, insofar as they restrict awareness to that of a single source of unchanging stimulation, also seem to produce the same effects. So we can say (within our frame of reference) that concentrative meditation is a practical technique which uses an experiential knowledge of the structure of our nervous system to "turn off" awareness of the external world and produce a state of blank-out or darkness, the "void," the cloud of unknowing. The techniques of concentrative meditation are not deliberately mysterious or exotic[29] but are simply a matter of practical applied psychology.

Chapter Two :

The Esoteric and Modern Psychologies of Awareness

These natural questions arise:

Why do these disciplines seem to share the common aim of "turning off" ordinary awareness of the external world for a short period of time?

What is the experience of meditators after that of "darkness"?

What are the general effects of the practice of meditation on awareness?'

What is the relationship of the "turning-off" form of meditation to the "opening-up" form?

With the viewpoint adopted in this essay, we may be able to provide appropriate answers to these questions.

If we are to determine the aftereffects of concentrative meditation on awareness, it would be useful to review some aspects of the psychology and physiology of consciousness. Though we should not expect that the practice of meditation will necessarily change every aspect of ordinary consciousness, we may be able to determine more clearly the effect and aftereffect of meditation in terms of our knowledge of the psychology and physiology of consciousness.

Contemporary psychology provides several different viewpoints from which to characterize awareness. Some are completely independent of one another, some are complementary, some intersect.

We normally consider that the single function of our sensory systems is to gather information about the world: we see with our eyes, we hear with our ears. Gathering information is certainly a major function of sensation, but sensory systems also act in just the opposite way. Our ordinary awareness of the world is selective and is restricted by the characteristics of sensory systems. Many philosophers have stressed a similar view, but only recently has precise physiological evidence been available. Huxley and Broad have elaborated on Bergson's general view of the mind as a "reducing valve." In ***The Doors of Perception and Heaven and Hell***, Huxley quotes Dr. D. C. Broad, the eminent Cambridge philosopher:

> *The function of the brain and nervous system is to protect us from being overwhelmed and confused by this mass of largely useless and irrelevant knowledge, by shutting out most of what we should otherwise perceive and remember at any given moment, leaving only that very small and special selection that is likely to be practically useful.*

And then Huxley comments:

> *According to such theory each one of us is potentially Mind at Large. But insofar as we are animals our business is at all costs to survive. To make biological survival possible, Mind at Large has to be funneled through the reducing valve of the brain and nervous system. What comes out at the other end is a measly trickle of the kind of consciousness which will help us to stay alive on the surface of this particular planet. To formulate and express the contents of this reduced awareness man has invented and endlessly elaborated those symbol-systems and*

implicit philosophies that we call languages. Every individual is at once the beneficiary and the victim of the linguistic tradition into which he has been born — the beneficiary inasmuch as language gives access to the accumulated records of other people's experience, the victim insofar as it confirms him in the belief that reduced awareness is the only awareness and it bedevils his sense of reality, so that he is all too apt to take his concept for data, his words for actual things. That which, in the language of religion, is called "this world" is the universe of reduced awareness expressed, and, as it were, petrified by language. The various "other worlds" with which human beings erratically make contact, are so many elements in the totality of awareness belonging to Mind at Large. Most people most of the time know only what comes through the reducing valve and is consecrated as genuinely real by their local language. Certain persons, however, seem to be born with a kind of bypass that circumvents the reducing valve. In others temporary bypasses may be acquired either spontaneously or as the result of deliberate "spiritual exercises" or through hypnosis or by means of drugs. Through these permanent or temporary bypasses there flows, not indeed the perception of everything that is happening everywhere in the universe (for the bypass does not abolish the reducing valve which still excludes the total content of Mind at Large), but something more than, and above all something different from, the carefully selected, utilitarian material which our narrow individual minds regard as a complete, or at least sufficient, picture of reality.[1]

Huxley writes more elegantly and less quantitatively than do most researchers and theorists in the fields of psychology and physiology, but much modern work in these disciplines tends to support the same general view that ordinary awareness is a personal construction. If awareness is a construction and not a "registration" of the external world, then by altering the nature of the construction process our awareness can be changed.

The normal view outside of the philosophical tradition, psychology, and the esoteric disciplines is that we experience *what exists,* that the external world is completely and perfectly reflected in our subjective experience. This idea is quite impossible to maintain even at the simplest level if we consider the many different forms of energy that impinge upon us at any moment. Sounds, electricity, light waves, magnetism, smells, chemical and electrical impulses within ourselves, thoughts, internal muscular sensations, all constantly bombard us. An appropriate question on the nature of our "ordinary" consciousness should be one that reflects a view quite different from the common one. How do we ever achieve a stable consciousness in the face of all this fantastic amount of stimulation?

There are two major ways in which we "make sense" out of the world. First, we use our sensory systems to discard and to simplify the incoming information, allowing only a few of the possible dimensions of sensation into our awareness. Second, we further sort the amount of information that does come in along a very limited number of dimensions, out of which we construct our awareness. These dimensions have been called in psychology "unconscious inferences," "personal constructs," "category systems," "efferent readinesses," or "transactions," depending on the writer's style and his level of analysis.

Quite obviously, each individual receptor is equipped physiologically to receive information only within certain limits. We wouldn't expect our eyes, for instance, to respond to the low bass note of an organ, or our ears to the taste of noodles. The eyes are "tuned" by their physiological structure to receive only a certain limited frequency range of stimulation and to send messages to the brain when energy in the appropriate frequency range reaches them — and so with the ears, the tongue, etc. That sensory receptors function to reduce the incoming information can be better understood if we study animals who are lower on the phylogenetic continuum and whose receptors discard even more information than do our own. It is difficult, otherwise, to conceive of the amount of stimulation to which we ourselves do not respond.

Perhaps the most cogent illustration of this point has been in the study of the visual system of the frog. The eye of the frog was studied by Lettvin, Maturana, McCulloch, and Pitts at the Massachusetts Institute of Technology. They were interested, essentially, in the same point made by Huxley, that sensory systems serve mainly for data *reduction.*[2]

They devised an experiment in which visual stimulation could be offered to one of the eyes of an immobilized frog. The frog was seated so that its eye was at the center of a hemisphere with a radius of seven inches. On the inner surface of this hemisphere small objects could be placed in different positions by means of magnets or moved around in space. The investigators implanted micro-electrodes into the frog's optic nerve to measure, as they called it, "what the frog's eye tells the frog's brain" — the electrical impulses sent to the brain by the eye. Since the frog's eye is somewhat similar to our own, these investigators hoped that electrical recording from the optic nerve would show the different kinds of "messages" that the eye sends to the brain. They studied the relationship of the evoked patterns of electrical activity to the different objects displayed on the hemisphere. There are thousands, millions, of different visual patterns that one could present to a frog — colors, shapes, movements, in various combinations, the almost infinite richness of the visual world of which we are normally aware. However, in presenting a large number of different objects, colors, movements, to the frog, a remarkable phenomenon was observed: from all the different kinds of stimulation presented only four different kinds of "messages" were sent from the retina to the brain. In other words, no matter the complexity and subtle differences in the environment, the frog's eye is "wired up" to send only this extremely limited number of different messages. The frog's eye presumably evolved to discard the remainder of the information available. The structure of its eye limits the frog's awareness to only four different kinds of visual activity. Lettvin and the others termed the four related systems: sustained contrast detectors; moving edge detectors; net dimming detectors; and net convexity detectors.

The first provides the general outline of the environment; the second seems to enhance response to sudden moving shadows, like a bird of prey; the third responds to a sudden decrease in light, a when a large enemy is attacking. These are systems that have presumably evolved to abstract information relevant to survival and to discard the rest, in the manner described by Huxley.

The fourth type of "message," conveyed by the net convexity detectors, is the most obviously related to survival and the most interesting of all. The net convexity detectors do not respond to any general change in light or to contrast; they respond only when small dark objects come into the field of vision, when these objects move at a closer distance, wriggling in front of the eye. It is quite clear, then, how the frog gets its food, how it can see flying bugs in front of it even with its limited visual system. The frog has evolved its own subsystem, which is wired up to ignore all other information except that of bugs flying around close to it — a very specialized "bug-perceiving" subsystem.

So, out of the complexity and richness of the information presented to the eye, the frog extracts only images with four dimensions. Higher-level animals exhibit similarities to this kind of process but on a much more complicated level. This type of dimensional analysis has been extended to cats and monkeys by David Hubel and Torstein Weisel at Harvard University and by many other investigators, who have determined that different cells in the brain respond to different types of stimulation. They found that certain cells detect edges and corners, others respond to movement on the retina, etc. Although vision has been the sensory system generally studied, since it is much easier to record from and much easier to specify what the dimension is, one would also expect that other sensory modalities would show the same kinds of relationships.

Sensory systems by "design" reduce the amount of useless and irrelevant information. We can then say that the function of our receptors and sensory systems is not only to gather information but to *select* and discard it.

If we consider more and more complicated organisms, their capacity to "retune" their sensory systems becomes greater. If the visual world of a goldfish is turned upside down by surgically inverting its eyes, it never learns to adjust to the new situation, swimming continually in a circle until death, or until a kind surgeon reorients its eyes. If the visual field of a human is turned around by wearing inverting lenses, he can, in a few weeks, perform actions as complicated as riding a bicycle through town. To make use of the familiar machine analogies, the sensory systems of some animals are like permanently wired-up simple machines. In a mousetrap or a pencil sharpener or even in a telephone or an automobile, a change in one part throws everything else out of adjustment, since it has no built-in capacity for self-alteration. As we consider more complicated animals, more and more advanced all the way up to man, their nervous systems seem to be more computer-like — machines, to be sure but ones that can alter the relationship between input and performance by a change in the "program." The higher mammals can be regarded as machines that are capable of "retuning" themselves in accordance with alterations in the external environment. This is not to say that there are no limits to their performance. Even the most sophisticated current computer has its physical limitations. No matter how the computer alters its own programs, it will never learn to fly. But it can alter itself within the limits of its own structure, as we can.

We can easily demonstrate this computer-like, higher-level selectivity and tuning. At a party or at a place where several people are talking at the same time, we close our eyes and listen to just one person speaking, then tune him out and listen to another person. We are able to do this, to listen to one person's speech and then suppress it as it comes into our ears and hear another person's speech that we have previously ignored. It is very easy to do. We shouldn't really be surprised since we tune ourselves continuously to suit our needs and expectations, but we are not usually aware of it. When we perspire during the summer we like the taste of foods that are more salty than usual. We don't think consciously that we need salt and we should take more salt in our foods; we *simply like* foods that at other times we would consider quite oversalted. The character in the middle of Figure 2 can be seen either as a number or as a letter depending upon the context, which governs how we tune ourselves.

Figure 2

Some examples from our everyday existence show how we become more sensitive to portions of our environment when we are in need. When we are hungry we see more restaurants, see more food, and smell more aromas than when we are not. When we are awaiting someone we immediately notice anyone who resembles the other person, in his hair color, general appearance, clothes, or because he is coming out of the door through which we expect the person to arrive. When we are interested in the opposite sex, we perceive them differently than when we are not. When after a meal our need for food has diminished, so does the attractiveness of food. We are able continuously to reprogram and reconstruct our awareness, based, at least in part, on our intent.

Many contemporary psychologists have investigated this "tuneability." Some have made use of a "tachistoscope," a visual display device that allows figures, objects, pictures, to be presented for short and measurable periods of time. One interesting series of experiments based on the tachistoscope demonstrated that we recognize familiar objects or words with less time exposure than unfamiliar ones. Our past experiences can tune input processing so that we can construct an image based on a small amount of input information. A coherent sentence, for instance, is much easier to recognize and to remember than just a random combination of words. Again, our past experience "tunes" us to have some idea of what should follow what, and we need much less information to construct an image. Jerome Bruner calls this "going beyond the information given."[3]

A major way in which we create our awareness is by tuning out the constancies in our environment. While we are learning a new skill, like skiing, all the complex adjustments and motor movements are somewhat painfully in our awareness. As we progress, as skill becomes "automatic," the movements no longer enter consciousness. Compare the first time you tried to drive a car, especially one with a gear shift, with how it feels to drive a car now, after you've learned. When we drive to work the first time, everything appears quite new and interesting — a red house, a big tree, the road itself — but gradually, as we drive the same route over and over, we "get used" to everything on the way. We stop "seeing" the trees, the bridges the corners, etc. We become "automatic" in our response to them. When we enter a room and a fan is turning, creating a buzzing sound, we are aware of it for the first few moments and then the sound seems to go out of awareness.

Many of the producers of the objects we buy take into account that we constantly need new stimulation, and that we adapt to and tune out the old. When we listen to a new song or piece of music, we play it over and over again for a period, and then leave it on the shelf unplayed. We get bored, the music no longer seems "new"; it is out of our awareness — on "automatic." Most of the market products are periodically changed slightly (automobiles, for instance), so that we begin to "see" them again, and presumably buy them.

In psychology and physiology, the phenomenon we have described is termed "habituation." The "response" in this case is one of the physiological components of the "orienting reaction" to new stimuli, the reaction that involves our registering of input. The physiological indicators of such reaction include EEG, heart rate, and skin resistance. Suppose we measure the resistance of the skin, for example, and repeat a click every five seconds. The first tone will cause a sharp drop in skin resistance. There will be less skin resistance change caused by the second tone, still less by the third, until, depending on the parameters of the particular experiment; the skin resistance no longer drops with each click. The response of the skin to this stimulus has been "habituated." When, after hearing for a while the sound of a clock ticking, we then tune the sound out, we no longer show the "orienting" or registering reaction. This does not merely involve a simple process of raising the threshold for stimuli entering into awareness and thus tuning the tick out. Our computer is capable of a more sophisticated selective tuning. It is true that if we substitute a louder tick, we will begin to hear it again. And if we substitute a *softer* one, the orienting reaction also returns and we will hear it again. If we change the interval between the appearances of the tick — if it appears a little bit later than we expect, or a little bit sooner, even slightly — the tick returns to our awareness, and the orienting reaction reappears.

Karl Pribram has pointed out another example of this phenomenon, which he called the "Bowery El" effect. In New York City an elevated railroad once ran along Third Avenue. At a certain time late each night a noisy train would pass through. The train line was torn down some time ago with some interesting aftereffects. People in the neighborhood called the police to report "something strange" occurring late at night — noises, thieves, burglars, etc. It was determined that these calls took place at around the time of the former late-night train. What these people were "hearing," of course, was the *absence* of the familiar noise of the train. We have a similar experience, although much simpler, when a noise that has been going on suddenly stops.[4]

If we look at the same object over and over again, we begin to look in the same way each time. We do this with the constancies of our world, our ordinary surroundings — the pictures in our house, the route we drive every day, etc. Charles Furst has studied the effect of repeated viewing of the same picture on the way we look at it.[5]

He found that eye movements tend to become more and more stereotyped as the same visual stimulus is presented. When we see a new image our eyes tend to move in a new pattern around it, but as we see it again and again, like the rooms in our house, we tend to look in a fixed way at fixed portions of it and ignore or tune out the rest. The "Bowery El" effect, the "Furst" effect, and the more precise studies of habituation suggest that we tune out the recurrences of the world by making a "model" of the external world within our nervous system, and testing input against it.[6] We somehow can program and continuously revise or reprogram conception or models of the external world. If the input and our model agree, as they do most often with the constancies of the world, then the input stays out of consciousness. If there is any disagreement, if the new input is *even slightly* different, slower, softer, louder, a different form, color, or even if it is absent, we become aware of the particular input once again. This "programming" forms an additional reducing valve behind the fixed reducing valves of the senses.

Perhaps the most clear and striking trend in the psychology and physiology of perception in the past few years has been our increasing understanding of the interactive and constructive nature of our "ordinary" awareness. One of the leaders in this investigation, Jerome Bruner, has emphasized that perception involves acts of categorization.[7] As we become experienced in dealing with the world we attempt to make more and more consistent "sense" out of the mass of information arriving at our receptors. We develop stereotyped systems or categories for sorting the input that reaches us. The set of categories we develop is limited, much more limited than the richness of the input. Simple categories may be "straight," "red," or "animal." More complex ones may be "English," "rectilinear," or "in front of." In social situations categories may be personality traits. If we come to consider a person "aggressive," we then consistently tend to sort all his actions in terms of this particular category. Personality traits seem to exist mainly in the category system of the perceiver.[8]

Our previous experience with objects strengthens our category systems. We expect cars to make a certain noise, traffic lights to be a certain color, food to smell a certain way, and certain people to say certain things. But what we actually experience, according to Bruner and to others, is the *category* which is evoked by a particular stimulus, and *not* the occurrence in the external world.

Bruner and his associates conducted an extensive series of studies on the effects of category systems on awareness. In his review ***On Perceptual Readiness***, he suggests that "correct" perception is

> *...not so much a matter of representation as it is a matter of what I shall call model-building. In learning to perceive we are learning the relations that exist between the properties of objects and events that we encounter and learning appropriate categories and category systems.* Learning to predict and

project what goes with what. *A simple example illustrates the point. I present for tachistoscopic recognition two nonsense words, one a zero-order approximation to English, constructed according to Shannon's rule, and a four-order approximation, W-R-U-L-P-Z-O-C and V-E-R-N-L-A-T, 500 ms of exposure one perceives correctly and in their place about 48 per cent of the letters in zero-order words. And about 93 per cent of the letters of the four-order words; ...the difference in perception is a function of the fact that individuals learn the traditional probability mode, what goes with what in English writing.* " [9]

Bruner, Postman, and Rodrigues attempted to demonstrate the effects of our well-learned categories on the contents of awareness.[10] They used ordinary playing cards familiar to most people in our culture. Our past experience with playing cards evokes categories in which the colors and the forms of playing cards are "supposed" to fall. We expect shapes like ♣ and ♠ to be black and ♦ and ♥ to be red.

Subjects in this experiment looked at the cards one at a time. A few of the cards were "anomalous," "wrong" colors for their shapes — a red ace of spades, a black eight of diamonds, etc. Subjects tended not to see the miscolored cards as anomalous, thus "correcting" the image. They would call a red ace of spades an ace of hearts, for instance. Not until it was expressly pointed out to the subjects that the colors might not necessarily, in this situation, be those usually associated with the shapes were the anomalous cards seen for what they were. The import of these and others of Bruner's interesting demonstrations is that we expect certain correspondences of objects, colors, forms, to occur, and we tune ourselves to see them. Newspaper editors often note that numerous typographical errors go unnoticed. The reader does the "correcting" within himself, merely by selecting the category "correct English."

At about the time Bruner was studying the effects of categories, another group of psychologists, led by Adelbert Ames, was exploring a similar viewpoint on the nature of awareness. Ames characterized the nature of ordinary awareness as a "transaction" between the perceiver and the environment. In spite of the overflow of information available to our sense organs at any given time, *relevant* information is often lacking. We cannot, for instance, determine tri-dimensionality directly. We cannot tell whether a room is "really" rectangular or not, or whether a given chair is physically closer than others, since we do not possess a direct sense of distance. There are, however, perceptible dimensions usually associated with closeness of objects. If we assume constant size, an image that seems larger is closer to us. So if we are trying to determine closeness, we "bet" that the larger object is the closer. That is, again, not a conscious process of correction. We *directly experience* the larger object as closer. The Ames group set out to demonstrate the nature of the bet we make with the environment.[11]

By manipulating our "unconscious inference," as Helmbolz called it, we can become aware of the bets or, in Bruner's term, the "categories" that constitute our awareness. To give another example, normally when we see a line drawing of a room as in Figure 3, we bet that in a top view it would be shaped like Figure 4, a rectangle. But a rectangle is only one of the many possible forms that could be derived from the two-dimensional drawing. One side may not be at all parallel with the other. The top view might look like either of the drawings in Figure 5, or any of many other shapes. We bet that the room is rectangular because almost all the rooms in our experience

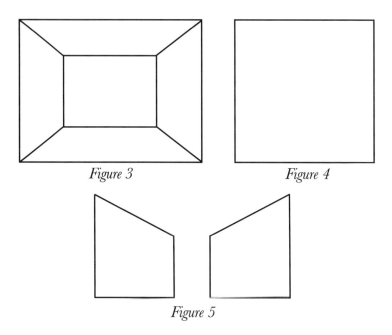

Figure 3   Figure 4

Figure 5

are rectangular. But if the room is not in fact rectangular, our bet causes us to "see" objects or people in the room in a very strange way. (*See Figure 6.*) George Kelly pursued a similar line of investigation, concerned more with the

Figure 6: The distorted room

psychology of ordinary experience and with clinical psychology. His conception was that each man creates his own world by means of his "personal constructs." He considered these "constructs" as scientific hypotheses, in that they are generated on the basis of our past experience and are applied to new experiences as long as they seem to work. So, for Kelly, our experience of the world consists of our constructs, as it consists of categories for Bruner and of transactions for the Ames group. Kelly was a psychotherapist and his therapy was based on the belief that a patient's problems were in large part due to his poor construction of the situation. The treatment involved a "prescription" of new constructions that the patient could apply to his life.[12]

There have been other studies along these general lines. Dr. Edward Sadalla and I attempted to test the effects of different constructs on the experience of duration. The experience of duration, of time lengthening or shortening, seems to be related to the amount of information that we "remember" as required by a given situation. We tried to alter the amount of information that a person would assume to be present in a constant situation. We made a film of a modern dancer performing several movements in a series. These movements were rather abstract to most people except modern dancers, and the interpretation could be easily altered. We trained one group of people to code the dance into two segments or constructs, another to code six segments, and a third, eleven segments. Those who were trained to code eleven segments (occurrences) perceived the dance as much longer than those who coded six, who in turn experienced the dance as longer than those who coded two.[13]

In a later study, Sadalla has shown that training to code different constructions has a basic effect on the recognition of various individual components of the dance.[14] Albert Hastorf and Hadley Cantril of the Ames group studied an even more complex effect. It is clear that we can tune ourselves on the basis of our needs and on the basis of our conception of past experience, and even on the basis of our expectation of future occurrences. Hastorf and Cantril demonstrated that people "tune" their perception on the basis of a quite complex expectation — by being "for" a team in a football game, for instance. The perception of the same events (a play in a football game, a verbal interchange) can be quite different in different people, depending upon these very general biasing factors, which can completely change the nature of the experience of a given series of events.

Since we can tune ourselves on the basis of our category systems, there must be physiological mechanisms that allow us to tune our awareness. Pribram and Spinelli have set out to demonstrate an analogue of this process on the physiological level.[15] They recorded from cells in the frontal cortex of the brain while stimulating other areas, and showed that the pattern of the receptive fields to external stimuli can be altered by the brain. The way in which stimuli are received, even as far out as on the retina itself, is "reprogrammable" on a moment-to-moment basis, and this can be demonstrated physiologically. These and other experiments demonstrate that the output system of the brain (efference) has an effect on the input (afference), the brain "selecting its input."

The investigation of the active role of the brain's output in determining the contents of awareness has been a major trend in the psychophysiology of perception. The work of Bruner, of the transactionists, and of Kelly demonstrate this active role on a psychological level; that of Pribram and Spinelli on the physiological. Some investigators have been explicitly concerned with the relationship between the input processing and the output systems of the brain in determining awareness. One test that we can try ourselves is that of closing one eye and pushing the other eye with a finger to a side. The visual world seems to "jump" a bit, it seems discontinuous. But if we make an eye movement in the usual manner over the same space, the world doesn't seem to jump. This difference indicates that in constructing our awareness we must also take our own movements into account and correlate them with the changes in input. If we didn't have a record somewhere of our efference, in this case our eye movements, the visual world would be constantly jumping around.

Some have gone so far as to maintain that consciousness depends *solely* upon the output of the brain, regardless of which input keys off a given output. Roger Sperry emphasized this point,[16] and later Taylor and Festinger provided some experimental demonstrations of this idea. Their statement that awareness depends solely on the output regardless of the input is not at all inconsistent with Bruner's contention that the category activated will determine awareness. In one case, if one is "ready" to see a black ace of spades or a red ace of hearts when a red ace of spades is shown, one will see one of the two choices one has set for himself. On the other hand, if one is "ready" to make a straight eye movement in response to a curved line, one will see the curved line as straight.

We ordinarily speak of "seeing an image" on the retina of our eyes. More properly, we do not really "see" with our eyes but, rather, with the help of our eyes. The eyes and other sense organs should be considered information selection systems. We can trick the eye, for instance, in several ways. If we press on our eyelids with our eyes closed, we "see" a white light, and yet there is no physical light energy present. What we have done is to cause the cells in the retina to fire by pressure instead of by their usual source of stimulation, light energy. The cells in the retina fire and send signals up to the brain. Messages from the retina are interpreted as light by the brain, no matter how the message was brought about, and so we are tricked into "seeing." There are times when we do not even need our eyes to "see" — for instance, when we dream at night or in the case of hallucinations, there is no light energy reaching our eyes.

Wilder Penfield, a Canadian neurosurgeon, has demonstrated the same point.[17] He performed brain surgery for patients with epilepsy and, as part of this procedure, electrically stimulated various areas of the brain. His patients would often report conscious experiences without any input at all. In addition, stimulation of the visual cortex usually leads to the experience of vision. We can understand, then, that seeing is not a process which takes place *in* our eyes but, rather, *with the help* of our eyes. It is a process that occurs in the brain and is determined by the category and output systems of the brain. Vision is a process that is fed only by the input that comes through our eyes, and our awareness is constructed from this input and from our past experience.[18]

Our eyes are also constantly in motion, in large eye movements (saccades) as well as in eye tremors (nystagmus). We blink our eyes every second, move our eyes around, move our heads, our bodies, and we follow moving objects. The view of an object is never constant, and the very receptive fields on the eyes are changing all the time. Yet our visual world remains very stable. We can walk around a horse, for instance, and although our view is constantly changing —

we sometimes see the tail, sometimes the back, a side view, a three-quarter view, a straight front view — we always see the same horse. If we "saw" an "image" on our retina, the visual world would be different each second. We must then *construct* our awareness from the selected input sorted into categories and in this way achieve some stability of our awareness out of the rich and continuously changing flow of information reaching our receptors.

We might briefly review some of these general characteristics of our awareness. Our senses receive information from the external world but, for the most part, are built to discard much of the continuously changing stimulation that reaches them. We also possess the ability to restrict further and modify the information that reaches awareness, by "reprogramming." The brain selects and modifies input. We build "models" or representations of the world based on our past experience. We can, therefore, tune our awareness on the basis of past experience, expectation, and needs. We use this ability to tune out the constancies of the world, the clock ticking, the route over which we normally drive, our living room, an old song. Our experience is therefore an interactive process between the external world and the continuously revised models of our categories. We can select input, tune ourselves to relevant input, categorize, and finally construct our awareness from these and from our past experiences, our associations, thoughts, and emotional state.

Similar analyses of normal awareness appear in literature. Lawrence Durrell's four novels of the **Alexandria Quartet** investigate the interactive nature of awareness. Durrell explores the same series of events as they appear to different people. For Durrell, as for Kelly, it is not important what actually happens, but what, rather, is construed to have happened. The world of Durrell's novels reflects the richness and complexity of life itself. In Akira Kurosawa's classic film **Rashômon** a woman is raped and her husband killed. The film gives us four viewpoints of the incident and we never know which version, if any, is 'the truth' about what happened.

The current work in American academic psychology provides a useful means of understanding normal awareness as a constructive process. One dimension, though, that is lacking in the current characterization is an analysis of the continuous flow of awareness. The writers cited provide a useful series of metaphors for the frame-by-frame components of awareness, but this is a segmented analysis. There is no doubt that at any instant our awareness is a construction based on past experience, but a more general characterization of the continuing nature of our awareness is needed. A more suitable metaphor was given by William James in his **Principles of Psychology**. He considered changing direction. James said:

> *Consciousness then does not appear to itself chopped up in bits. Such words as chain or train do not describe it fitly, as it presents itself in the first instant. It is nothing joined, it flows, a river or a stream are the metaphors by which it is naturally described. In talking of it thereafter, let us call it the stream of thought, of consciousness, or of subjective life.*[19]

Our thoughts are in constant change. Awareness shifts from one aspect of the stimuli surrounding us to another, to a thought of the past, to a bodily sensation, to a plan, to a change in external stimulation, back and forth. The stream carves its own new path continuously. James would have agreed with the more recent and precise analysis that awareness is a simplification and a construction. He said:

Looking back, then, over this review, we see that the mind is at every stage a theatre of simultaneous possibilities. Consciousness consists in the comparison of these with each other, the selection of some, and the suppression of others, of the rest by the reinforcing and inhibiting agency of attention. The highest and most celebrated mental products are filtered from the data chosen by the faculty next beneath, out of the mass offered by the faculty below that, which mass was in turn sifted from a still larger amount of yet simpler material, and so on. The mind, in short, works on the data it received much as a sculptor works on his block of stone. In a sense, the statue stood there from eternity. But there were a thousand different ones beside it. The sculptor alone is to thank for having extricated this one from the rest. Just so the world of each of us, however different our several views of it may be, all lay embedded in the primordial chaos of sensations, which gave the mere matter to the thought of all of us indifferently. We may, if we like, by our reasoning unwind things back to that black and jointless continuity of space and moving clouds of swarming atoms which science calls the only real world. But all the while the world we feel and live in will be that which our ancestors and we, by slowly cumulative strokes of choice, have extricated out of this, like sculptors, by simply rejecting certain portions of the given stuff. Other sculptors, other statues from the same stone! Other minds, other worlds, from the same monotonous and inexpressive chaos! My world is but one in a million, alike embedded and alike real to those who may abstract them. How different must be the world in the consciousness of ants, cuttlefish or crab! [20]

A similar characterization of awareness is offered by the Indian yogi, Vivikenanda. He more negatively compares ordinary awareness to a "drunken monkey." He calls up images of awareness moving from one random thought to another — thinking about hunger, thinking about the past, glimpsing an aspect of the present, thinking of the future, planning an action — continuously bouncing around like a monkey from one thing to another.

The esoteric traditions in general have characterized consciousness in terms similar to those of modern psychology. The Sufis are the clearest precursors of modern psychology's conceptions of awareness. Sufi teaching stories frequently focus on men who are too preoccupied to hear what is being said, or who misinterpret instruction because of their expectations, or who do not see what is in front of them, because of the limited nature of their constructs.[21] The Sufis emphasize the constantly changing biases that constitute our normal awareness. "What a piece of bread looks like depends on whether you are hungry," says a Sufi poet, Jalaluddin Rumi. The Sufis quite explicitly consider the effects of our limited category system on awareness. Many of the Sufis' descriptions of awareness could have been a statement of Bruner's about category systems, or a summary by Lettvin of his research on the frog, e.g., "Offer a donkey a salad, and he will ask what kind of thistle it is." They emphasize that we can be aware of only that which we conceive to exist, and that which our senses will transmit to us.

The Sufi and other traditions contend that the selective and restricted nature of awareness is an obstacle to be overcome and that the process of meditation, among other exercises, is a way of turning down the restrictions that normally limit awareness. One specific aim in these traditions is the removal of the automaticity and selectivity of ordinary awareness. The Sufis characterize man's usual state as one of "deep sleep" or "blindness," as one of being concerned with the irrelevant dimensions of the world. Gurdjieff's image is that of man placing shock absorbers between himself and the world. "We must destroy our buffers, children have none, therefore we must become like little children."[22] In Indian thought, as we have seen, ordinary awareness is a "drunken monkey" living solely in his constructs — the world of "illusion." This same thought is the metaphorical meaning of the "fall" of man in the Christian tradition. All these metaphors, without their derogatory connotation, can be understood in terms of modern psychology as depicting our selective awareness, our model-building, our automaticity, and our limited category systems.

An aim of meditation, or more generally of the disciplines involving meditation, is the removal of "blindness," or the illusion, and an "awakening" of "fresh" perception. Enlightenment or illumination are words often used for progress in these disciplines, for a breakthrough in the level of awareness — flooding a dark spot with light. The Indian tradition speaks of opening the third eye, seeing more, and from a new vantage point. *Satori*, the desired state in Zen, is considered an "awakening." The Sufis speak of growing a new organ of perception.

Reports of the experiences of practitioners of the disciplines of meditation indicate that a primary aftereffect of the concentrative meditation exercises is an "opening up" of awareness, a "deautomatization," as Deikman calls it, which may be considered as involving a reduction of the processing of input. Deikman's own subjects, who gazed at a blue vase for a half-hour at a time over a number of sessions, reported that the vase appeared "more vivid" and "more luminous."[23] Deikman quotes Augustine Poulain, who emphasized that concentrative meditation is a temporary process of withdrawal, a blank-out, in other terms, of awareness with the intent to become deautomatized or dishabituated.

It is the mysterious darkness wherein is contained the limitless Good. To such an extent are we admitted and absorbed into something that is one, simple, divine, and illuminable that we seem no longer distinguishable from it...In this unity the feeling of multiplicity disappears. When afterwards these persons come to themselves again, they find themselves possessed of a more distinct knowledge of things, some luminous and more perfect than that of others.[24]

Some speak of seeing things "freshly" or as if for the first time. To William Blake, "if the doors of perception were cleansed, everything would appear to man as it is, infinite." Others, like Gurdjieff, use a loose metaphor and compare their experiences to that of a child who presumably has not yet developed many automatic ways of tuning out the world. In Zen, one speaks similarly of seeing something the five hundredth time in the same way one saw it the first time.

All of these descriptions are understandable and easily translatable into the more precise psychological terms of building a model of the environment and testing and selecting input against the model. When we see something for the five hundredth time we have developed a model for it and tune out the input.

These characterizations of consciousness represent a point of encounter between the concepts of contemporary psychology and the metaphors of the esoteric disciplines. We speak of man as controlling his input, building models, responding "automatically" to the external environment. The esoteric traditions refer to this process as man's lacking awareness of his surroundings and consider this "blindness" the barrier to his development. The practice of meditation, then, can be considered as an attempt to turn off conceptual activity temporarily, to shut off all input processing for a period of time, to get away for a while from the external environment.

A result of this "turning off" of our input selection systems is that, when we introduce the same sensory input later, we see it differently, "anew."

When we leave our normal surroundings and go on a vacation we usually return to find ourselves much more aware of the immediate environment. We play many of our old music or songs, which we haven't "heard" in a while. We look anew at the plants in our garden, the paintings on our walls, our friends. Getting away and returning seems to have the same effect on awareness as presenting new stimuli.*

We can consider the process of meditation as similar to that of taking a vacation — leaving the situation, "turning off" our routine way of dealing with the external world for a period, later returning to find it "fresh," "new," "different," our awareness "deautomatized."

Contemporary psychology recognizes that we easily adapt to most anything new. New technology, the changes in our environment, quickly becomes an integral part of our lives, part of our model. The model-building process is specifically what is to be dismantled through the practice of meditation. In Zen, one is instructed to stop conceptualizing while remaining fully awake. In Yoga, the aim is to leave the "illusion" — to cease identifying the external world with our models.

The three major traditions that we've considered each speak of developing an awareness that allows every stimulus to enter into consciousness devoid of our normal selection process, devoid of normal tuning and normal

---

*cf. the phenomenon of "spontaneous recovery" in habituation.

input selection, model-building, and the normal category systems.

The same metaphor is used in many traditions to describe the desired state of awareness. The Sufi poet Omar Khayyám says: "I am a mirror and who looks at me, whatever good or bad he speaks, he speaks of himself." The contemporary Zen master, Suzuki Roshi says: "The perfect man employs his mind as a mirror, it grasps nothing, it refuses nothing, and it receives but does not keep." Christ said in prayer: "A mirror I am to thee that perceivest me." The metaphor of consciousness as a mirror fits well with some of the psychologists' own metaphors. A mirror allows every input to enter equally, reflects each equally, it cannot be tuned to receive a special kind of input. It does not add anything to the input and does not turn off repetitive stimuli; it does not focus on any particular aspect of input and retune back and forth, but continuously admits all inputs equally.

This metaphor leads to another consideration. Many of the traditions claim to allow men to experience the world *directly*. The Sufis speak of attaining an "objective consciousness," others of "cosmic consciousness," and the statement is often made that one can have *direct* perception of reality. Whether one can perceive "reality" directly is not yet a question for science, but some comment within the terms of psychology might be made. The ability to be a mirror, to be free of the normal restrictions, of the tuning, biasing, and filtering processes of awareness, may be part of what is indicated by "direct" perception. This state can perhaps be considered within psychology as a diminution of the interactive nature of awareness; a state in which we do not select, nor do we bet on the nature of the world, nor do we think of the past, nor do we compel awareness by random associations, nor do we think of the future, nor do we set into restrictive categories, but a state in which all possible categories are held in awareness at once. It has been described also as living totally in the present; not thinking about the future or of the past; a state in which everything that is happening in the present moment enters into awareness.

There have been some studies of the state of awareness of practitioners in and after mediation. These studies have used the EEG to measure the response of the brain of meditators to the external stimulation.

When we enter a room and hear a clock ticking we ordinarily learn to tune it out fairly quickly. If we study this process physiologically, the normal orienting response to new stimulation would begin to disappear after a few moments and wouldn't reappear. We would have built a model to tune it out.[25] The response would have habituated. But if one's consciousness were like a mirror, then each time the clock ticked we would "reflect" the tick.

The Indian psychologists' studies on Yoga meditation showed this result. In testing the yogi's brain response to external stimuli, the current contention on the effects and aftereffects of meditation was confirmed. During the meditation and during the withdrawal there was no response in the yogi's brain to external stimuli. When the yogi was not meditating, repetition of the external stimulus showed no habituation, as it presumably would have occurred in other subjects.[26]

The Japanese neuropsychiatrists Kasumatsu and Hirai studied the habituation of the orienting response to a repeating click in ordinary people and in Zen masters. The subjects in this experiment sat in a soundproof room and listened to a click repeated each fifteen seconds while an EEG was being taken. The normal subjects showed the customary phenomenon of habituation. There was a decrease in the response of the brain's electrical activity to the click after the third or fourth click. After habituation, each time the click occurred there was no response in the brain of the subject: the click had been tuned out of awareness. When the Zen masters were exposed to this same repetitive click over a period of five minutes, they did not show the customary habituation but responded to the last click in the same way as they did to the first.[27] They did not seem therefore to make a "model" of the repetitive stimulation and tune it out.

There are important differences in intent in the particular forms of Zen and Yoga meditation, which would lead us to expect different kinds of responses to the external world during the meditation exercise and after. The early and beginning forms of Zen arc similar to Yoga; the breath counting, the koan, etc., involve an attempt to restrict awareness to a single process. We remember that Rahula indicates that one will not be aware of the external world if one does the breath-counting meditation successfully. These exercises are similar to the use of the mandala, mantra, mudra, etc., in Yoga. In the more advanced forms of Zen, in the Soto sect, once the breath-counting is mastered, the second form of meditation exercises, *shikan-taza*, is practiced — "just sitting." Yasutani Roshi describes this exercise as follows:

Up to now you have been concentrating on following your breaths with your mind's eye, trying to experience vividly the inhaled breath as only inhaled breath and the exhaled breath as only exhaled breath. From now on I want you to practice shikan-taza, *which I will shortly describe in detail...*

Shikan *means "nothing but" or "just," while ta means "to hit" and za "to sit." Hence shikan-taza is a practice in which the mind is intensely involved in just sitting. In this type of Za-Zen it is all too easy for the mind, which is not supported by such aids as counting the breath or by a koan, to become distracted. The correct temper of mind therefore becomes doubly important. Now,* in shikan-taza *the mind must be unhurried yet at the same time firmly planted or massively composed, like Mount Fuji let us say. But it also must be alert, stretched, like a taut bowstring. So* shikan-taza *is a heightened state of concentrated awareness wherein one is neither tense nor hurried, and certainly never slack. It is the mind of somebody facing death. Let us imagine that you are engaged in a duel of swordsmanship of the kind that used to take place in ancient Japan. As you face your opponent, you are unceasingly watchful, set, ready. Were you to relax your vigilance even momentarily, you would be cut down instantly. A crowd gathers to see the fight. Since you are not blind you see them from the corner of your eye, and since you are not deaf you hear them. But not for an instant is your mind captured by these sense impressions.*

This state cannot be maintained for long — in fact, you ought not to do shikan-taza *for more than half an hour at a sitting. After thirty minutes get up and walk around in* kinhin *[Zen moving meditation] and then resume your sitting. If you are truly doing* shikan-taza, *in half an hour you will be sweating, even in winter in an unheated room, because of the heat generated by this intense concentration. When you sit for too long, your mind loses its vigor, your body tires, and your efforts are less rewarding than if you had restricted your sitting to thirty-minute periods.*[28]

We can then consider two basic types of meditation exercises — both concerned with a common effect — those which "turn off" input processing for a period of time to achieve an *aftereffect* of "opening up" of awareness, and those which consist in the active practice of "opening up" during the period of the exercise.

To return for a moment to the studies of the response of Zen and Yoga meditators to external stimuli, we can expect dishabituation *during* the advanced form of Zen meditation — that is, a consistent response to a stimulus which continues — and a shutting down of awareness of external stimuli during Yoga meditation. When the yogin is not in meditation, we might expect no habituation to a repetitive stimulus (if he is advanced enough in his practice).

Active practice in opening up awareness is a part of all the traditions, but in Zen it is a specific meditation exercise. A less demanding Buddhist practice stems from one component of the Buddha's Eightfold Path and is usually termed "right-mindedness." It requires that one be "conscious" of everything one does, to attend very closely to ordinary activities, and to open up awareness to these activities while engaged in them. Rahula says:

> *Another very important, practical and useful form of "meditation" (mental development) is to be aware and mindful of whatever you do, physically or verbally, during the daily routine of work in your life, private, public or professional. Whether you walk, stand, sit, lie down or sleep, whether you stretch or bend your limbs, whether you look around, whether you put on your clothes, whether you talk or keep silent, whether you eat or drink — even whether you answer the calls of nature — in these and other activities you should be fully aware and mindful of the act performed at the moment, that is to say, that you should live in the present moment, in the present action. This does not mean that you should not think of the past or the future at all. On the contrary, you should think of them in relation to the present moment, to the present action, when and where this is relevant. People do not generally live in their actions in the present moment. They live in the past or the future. Though they seem to be doing something now here, they live somewhere else in their thoughts, in their problems and worries, usually in the memories of the past or in desires and speculations about the future. Therefore, they do not live*

in nor do they enjoy what they do at the moment, so they are unhappy and discontented with the present moment with the work at hand. Naturally, they cannot give themselves fully to what they appear to be doing.[29]

Spiegelberg gives an example of a similar practice in the Tibetan tradition. The Tibetan "Stories of the 84 Magicians" exercises, analogous to those described by Rahula, deal for the most part with the daily occupation of the mediator.

The street cleaner has to take his task of sweeping as the starting point for meditation. So, likewise, must the potter take his task of producing clay utensils on his potter's wheel and the cobbler, his handicrafts. Here, again, therefore, it is evident that one may do what he will so long as he is clearly aware of what he is doing. Every activity is of equal value as a basis for a dharana exercise.[30]

In Yoga, self-observation is called "the Witness." The attempt is to observe oneself as if one were another person. One tries to notice exactly what one is doing — to invest ordinary activity with attention. The witness does not judge action or initiate action. The witness simply observes.

In Zen, this practice is highly developed. Right-mindedness or attention to what one is doing can be a part of almost any activity that one performs, no matter how degrading. There is no action that cannot be used for the purposes of the alteration of one's consciousness. One simply need be mindful of what one is doing. One can be performing actions that are quite degrading to a Buddhist, such as butchering an animal, but simply by paying close attention to what one is doing, one's awareness can be developed.

In Sufism, at least in the version that is attributed to Gurdjieff, there are similar practices, one of which is called "self-remembering." As in Zen, no special constraints are put on action. There are no prohibitions as to what can be eaten or general rules of conduct. The attempt is simply to be aware of oneself. Gurdjieff's students are constantly instructed to "remember themselves" wherever they are, remember that they are present, and notice what they do. When one is "remembering oneself" in Gurdjieff's terms one is considered to be "awake." [31]

A similar exercise attributed to Gurdjieff consists simply in maintaining continuous awareness on a part of one's body — an elbow, hand, leg. Another exercise of this tradition is to perform ordinary habitual actions slightly differently, such as putting shoes on in the opposite order, shaving the other side of the face first, eating with the left hand. These can be seen as attempts to return the habitual "automatic" actions into full awareness.

Recall the phenomenon of habituation. A slight change in the input is enough to "dishabituate" and to return the stimulus to awareness. Similarly, slightly altering our usual "automatic" behavior, such as tying shoes or driving cars, can return it again into awareness.

In Yoga itself there is a tradition called *Karma Yoga*. The attempt is to treat everyday activities as a sacrament and to give them full attention. This exercise performs a function similar to "right-mindedness" and "self-remembering," and is perhaps a less extreme version of *shikan-taza*.

Many schools within these traditions combine the two major awareness exercises devoting a half-hour or so twice a day to the "shutting-down" form of meditation and as much as possible of the remainder of the day to a form of self-observation.

We mentioned earlier that the other major practice which often accompanies both forms of meditation is that of a renunciation of or a non-attachment to external objects. There are several different types of these practices, involving either prohibitions on behavior or the cultivation of a psychological state that combines renunciation and non-attachment. In the Judeo-Christian tradition, these practices usually involve behavioral restrictions. For example, some churchgoers are required during Lent to abstain from eating meat. The usual result of this kind of practice is that awareness is focused on the forbidden object. Most people find themselves craving meat, thinking about it, devising substitutes (meatless meals, for instance), waiting until the period of prohibition is over.

But the practice of renunciation, according to the various esoteric traditions, is intended to create a psychological state of *cessation*, not enhancement, of desire, and it is not necessarily tied to any change in external behavior. Most of the traditions emphasize that merely abstaining in practice while desiring, planning to consume the object, is worthless — perhaps worse than not giving it up at all. Christ himself made this point, although his followers do not always seem to be mindful of it.

Renunciation is the process, it is said, of conquering desire, of not requiring or needing anything. The Indian practices emphasize the cultivation of a psychological state of non-attachment as well as prohibitions on actual behavior. Most yogis are vegetarian, chaste, and live in poverty. Often yogic practice involves a withdrawal from society and its "temptations" into an *ashram*, in which one lives as a monk on a simple diet. Christian monasteries also emphasize psychological non-attachment as well as the actual cessation of certain "impure" behavior — the vows of poverty, chastity, solitude — a separation from the culture in order to "purify" oneself.

In the Zen and Sufi traditions the emphasis is solely on the psychological state of non-attachment and not on prohibitions in actual practice. Both Zen and Sufism emphasize, as they do in the exercise of self-awareness, that one can do whatever one wants as long as one is not attached to it.

The difference between the Sufis and Zen on the one hand, and much of Yoga and Christian tradition on the other, is illustrated in some advice given to Rafael Lefort, who traveled to the Mideast in search of the teachers of Gurdjieff — the Sufis — and was asked:

"Are you prepared to leave the world as you know it and live in a mountain retreat on a very basic diet?" I signified that I was.

"You see," he nodded his head regretfully, "you still feel that to find knowledge you must seek a solitary life away from impure things. This is a primitive attitude and one satisfactory for savages...Can you comprehend the uselessness of abandoning the world for the sake of your selfish development?

"You may need a course," he went on, "at a Sarmoun Centre, but that will not mean total abandonment of your mundane worldly activity provided you do not allow it, nay invite it, to corrupt you. If you have enough skill you can actually harness the negative forces to serve you...but you must have enough skill." [32]

Zen also points out that "worldly" activity can be a perfect vehicle for development as long as one is free from attachment. Worldly activity and pleasures are legitimate in Zen as long as one is not in their service. The Sufis admonition is: "Be *in* the world but not *of* the world." The attempt is to isolate the important aspect of renunciation, the psychological state of "non-attachment," from the external behavior. This is illustrated by a student's experience with Gurdjieff, when she felt that she was a "slave" to her habit of cigarette smoking. Gurdjieff, who stressed that men were often the slaves of their habits, instructed her to give up smoking. On returning to him a year later, she told Gurdjieff triumphantly that she had given up smoking and was no longer a slave to her cigarette habit. Gurdjieff smiled and immediately offered her a very expensive Turkish cigarette, indicating that it was not her behavior but the fact that she had been slave to her cigarette habit that was important. Only when she no longer needed to smoke was it permissible to smoke again.[22] Gurdjieff himself kept a quite well-known larder stocked with delicacies from all parts of the world.

But why is non-attachment to "worldly" pleasures a major part of the meditative disciplines? One answer can be given in terms of our analysis of ordinary consciousness. Recall that normal consciousness is constructed from our past experience, our expectations, and our needs. When we are hungry we are likely to search out food, or to *create* food images or smells, or to enhance food images that are present, or to think about food. A Sufi tale illustrates this general point:

> *Two men were sitting in a cafe and a camel walked past.*
> *"What does that make you think of?" said one.*
> *"Food," said the other.*
> *"Since when are camels used for food?" said the first*
> *"No, you see, everything makes me think of food."* [34]

The meditative traditions consider that one major barrier to the development of expanded awareness is that we continuously tune out those portions of the external environment that do not suit our needs at the moment. If we are hungry we would be very unlikely to notice the river around us or the people whom we see. We are concerned solely with food and construct our world around food.

In its effect on awareness, the practice of non-attachment can be considered as an additional way to remove the normal restrictions on input. If there are no desires, there is less of a bias at any one moment to "tune" perception. Our awareness of the external environment becomes less restricted, less of an interaction, less solely a function of our desire at the moment, and more like a mirror.

There is another function of non-attachment. If, for instance, one *needs* nothing from another person or from the external environment — prestige, sex, food, love — one can exist "for them" as a mirror, as do Omar Khayyám, Suzuki Roshi, and Christ. We sometimes approach this state when we feel free of conventional social obligations.

A more extreme example can be observed in the sensualist who is often the one who becomes the renunciant, a "worldly" man who gives up all for his religion — a Thomas à Becket.

In many ways the aims of the disciplines of meditation — total attention to the moment, "dishabituation," "extended" awareness — are the same ones we seek in many of our "ordinary" activities. We buy new products, new clothes, new music; we slightly change our surroundings to attempt to return them to awareness. Dangerous sports, for example, engage our awareness and bring us into the present moment in which we think of nothing else but the activity in which we are engaged. We arrange the conditions so that it is *absolutely necessary* for us to pay full attention to what is taking place at the moment. When we race a sports car or motorcycle, or ski or ride a toboggan down a slope, or sky-dive, anything less than complete awareness to the moment may lead to injury or to death. The necessity of opening up our awareness is perhaps one of the reasons people are willing to risk injury or even their lives in dangerous sports. A particularly good example is the sort of rock climbing that requires intense concentration over a prolonged period of time. Doug Robinson writes in **Ascent**, the journal of the Sierra Club: *

>...to take a familiar example, it would be hard to look at Van Gogh's "The Starry Night" without seeing the visionary quality in the way the artist sees the world. He has not painted anything that is not in the original scene, yet others would have trouble recognizing what he has depicted. The difference lies in the intensity of his perception, at the heart of his visionary experience, he is painting from a higher state of consciousness. Climbers too have their "starry nights." Consider the following from an account by Alan Steck of the Hummingbird Ridge Club on Mount Logan. "I turned for a moment and was completely lost in silent appraisal of the beautifully sensuous simplicity of windblown snow. The beauty of that moment, the form and motion of the blowing snow was such a powerful impression, and so wonderfully sufficient that the climber was lost in it. It is said to be only a moment and yet by virtue of total absorption he is lost in it and the winds of eternity blow through it!"
>
>A second example comes from an account of the 7th day and the 8th day of the first ascent under trying conditions on El Capitan's Muir Wall. Yvon Chouinard relates, in the 1966 American Alpine Journal: "...with our more receptive senses we now appreciated everything around us. Each individual

<hr>

*I would like to thank Dr. E. K. Sadalla for pointing this example out to me.

crystal in the granite stood out in bold relief. The varied shape of the clouds never ceased to attract our attention. For the first time we noticed tiny bugs that were all over the walls, so tiny they were barely noticeable. While belaying, I stared at one for fifteen minutes, watching him move and admiring his brilliant red color. How could one ever be bored with so many good things to see and feel? This unity with our joyous surroundings, this ultra penetrating perception gave us a feeling of contentment that we had not had for years."

In these passages the quality that makes up the climber's visionary experience are apparent: the overwhelming beauty of most ordinary objects — as clouds, granite, and snow — of his experience, the sense of the slowing down of time to the point of disappearing, and the "feeling of contentment" and an oceanic feeling of supreme sufficiency of the present, and while delicate in substance these feelings are still strong enough to intrude firmly into the middle of dangerous circumstances, and remain there temporarily superceding even apprehension and the drive for achievement.[35]

Much of Western art is similarly an attempt to "cleanse" perception, to return our awareness to things that are seen automatically. One critic considers the function of art to "make strange" ordinary objects, to allow us to see our usual surroundings as if they were "strange" — as if for the first time. The trend in Pop Art is an example. There is an important difference in the way we look at a Warhol sculpture of a Campbell's soup can in a gallery and at the same object at home. By presenting ordinary objects in a context that demands that we attend to them, we "see" them in a new way. We do not immediately call up our customary category of "soup can," in which we ignore everything but the particular label ("is it vegetable or noodle?"). We now "look" at the shape, the lettering, the way the light falls on the surface of the can. We are brought out of our ordinary responses of ignoring the object. Looking at a common object in a gallery is a means of deautomizing our awareness of it.

We could give many more examples from the fields of art, music, and literature. There are many essayists and poets who have written directly about meditative experiences and traditions; among them, William Blake, Herman Hesse, Aldous Huxley, T. S. Eliot; but it would be useful here to consider a writer whose work is quite different and who is not usually associated with this subject.

The sensualist Henry Miller would seem to share little with Huxley, Hesse, Eliot, the traditions of meditation, the rock climber, or the visual artist. But, in a volume of **The Rosy Crucifixion (Sexus)**, Miller states the aim of his work and life in terms almost identical to those of the esoteric traditions, namely, that men are "blind" and have first to acquire "vision."

...the world is not to be put in order: the world is order incarnate. It is for us to put ourselves in unison with this order, to know what is the world order and in contradistinction to the wishful thinking orders that we seek to impose on one another. The power which we long to possess in order to establish the good, the true and the beautiful would prove to be, if we could have it, but the means of destroying one another. It is fortunate that we are powerless. We have first to acquire vision, then discipline and forbearance until we have the humility to acknowledge a vision beyond our own, and until we have faith and trust in superior powers, the blind must lead the blind. Men who believe that work and brains will accomplish must ever be deceived by the quixotic and every unforeseen turn of events.[36]

In the ***World of Sex***, Miller makes the point, which could have been made by a Zen monk, that any ordinary activity, if one is mindful (in the Zen sense), can lead to a breakthrough. He also recalls Spiegelberg's comments that "every hallucination, every unappeasable hatred, every amorous attachment provides a certain power of concentration to him who cherishes it and helps to direct the forces of his being to a similar goal."

> *Life moves on whether we act as cowards or heroes. Life has no other discipline to impose, if we could but realize it, but to accept life unquestioningly. Everything we shut our eyes to, everything we run away from, everything we deny, denigrate or despise, serves to defeat us in the end. What seems nasty, painful, evil can become a source of beauty, joy, and strength if faced with an open mind. Every moment is a golden one for him who has the vision to recognize it as such. Life is now, every moment, no matter if the world be full of death. Death triumphs only in the service of life.*[37]

In ***"Creative Death"*** Miller writes:

> *Strange as it may seem today to say, the aim of life is to live, and to live is to be aware, joyously, drunkenly, divinely, serenely aware. In this state of godlike awareness one sings, and in this realm the world exists as poem, no why or wherefore, no direction, no goal, no striving, no revolving. Like the enigmatic Chinaman, one is rapt by the ever-changing spectacle of changing phenomenon; this is the sublime, the amoral state of the artist, he who lives only in the moment, the visionary moment of utter far-seeing lucidity. Such clear icy sanity that it seems like madness.* * [38]

---

*I was beginning to wonder whether the contention that much of our endeavors are directed to the same end as that of the disciplines

Although many of our endeavors are directed toward achieving a meditation-like state of awareness, these means are held to be inefficient by the esoteric traditions. If we actually do achieve states of total awareness to the moment by ordinary means, this achievement does not last for long, does not carry with it permanence. Our success fades, our love ends, we must come down from the mountain.

Noting the common aim of many of our interests and that of the disciplines of meditation, another function of detachment becomes more clear. The practice can be seen

of meditation is exaggerated. Perhaps I was forcing some of these into a mold. Then I happened to pick up two of the most popular magazines in this country, Life and Look, and read them at about the same time as this chapter was being prepared. In Life we read, in the introduction to a photographic essay; "Imprisoned in the narrowness of our human scale, we are blind to the vast reaches of reality. Mysteries lie all around us, even within us, waiting to be revealed by a new way of seeing." Then, in Look magazine: "Up, quick if you can it's long past time to do. You've stayed so long you've lost yourself and now exist cut off from all that is around you, from all of you that's human, you're civilized beyond your senses: out of touch, narcotized, mechanized, Westernized, with bleached out eyes that yearn for natural light. The intellects turn tyrant on us all and make our daily lives neatly laid-out, over-intellectualized, over-technological exercises in sinister lunacy. ...We are severed from ourselves and alien to our sensibilities, fragmented, specialized, dissected, and pigeon-holed into smothering." In popular music, a friend recalled the Beatles' song "Tomorrow Never Knows," which begins, "Turn off your mind, relax and float downstream,/it is not dying,/lay down all thoughts, surrender to the void/that you may see the meaning of within/it is shining."

as an attempt to separate the subjective state produced by sports, sex, love, music, art, etc., from that of its usual object, and to detach the effect — the resultant internal state — from the usual cause, the stimulus object. The person works then within himself to attempt to generate the internal state directly. "What need have I of an external woman when I have an internal woman," says a practitioner of *tantra*. The "worldly" sensualist perhaps sees the same possibility — to achieve a result that is similar to what he seeks in sensual activity, but one more permanent and under his control. He then gives up the outward manifestations of what he is seeking. The process involves a detachment from the usual triggers to this state — sex, love, prestige, power, money, food, etc. — and an attempt to concentrate upon internal "centers," which are held to give rise to these and to "higher" experiences. The energy force is called *kundalini* in Yoga, and these centers termed *chakras* in Yoga and *lataif* in the Sufi tradition. There are some differences in the two systems but these two centers are for this consideration analogous.* [39]

In the terms of this essay, detachment and concentration on these internal centers can be considered as an attempt to stimulate internally the structures that are usually associated with the experiences of dishabituation, pleasure, etc. We can consider the process as learning to stimulate the "reward" circuits on the brain.

Physiologists working with animals have implanted electrodes in those parts of the brain in which stimulation seems to serve as a reward, and they have had interesting results. In a situation where animals can continue the stimulation of these systems themselves, they will do so at

---

This energy system is not at all understood in science. The exercises are almost always given a secret and little is ever written of them.

the expense of everything else. Some actually worked to stimulate these circuits until they died, even though food and drink were available freely. They had no need of external stimulation because they could do it internally.[40] The second function of renunciation and the concomitant concentration on various parts of the body can then be considered as a functional training technique in self-stimulation of the centers of the nervous system.[41]

These first two sections of this essay have covered a lot of ground, so it should be of some use to recall briefly some of their major points.

If we ignore our preconceptions about the function of meditation and overcome both attraction and repulsion toward the exotic and esoteric, it is clear that the practices of meditation can be analyzed in terms of modern psychology. The repetitive or concentrative form of meditation can be seen as an exercise in "turning off" awareness of the external environment, inducing a central state in the nervous system equivalent to that of no external stimulation. In the traditions we are considering, this state is known as the "void" or the "darkness." If restriction of awareness is accomplished by other means, such as that of a ganzfeld, there is a similar result — the "blank-out" of experience of the external environment.

The production of a state in which one is insulated from the external world has some consistent aftereffects on awareness. Many meditators report seeing the world "anew," "fresh," seeing everything "glows," illuminated, enlightened. A metaphor used in most traditions for this state is that of a "mirror."

It is interesting to note the similarities between the esoteric and the modern psychologies of consciousness. Both stress that our awareness of the environment is a process of selection and categorization, that our sensory systems serve the purpose of discarding much of the information that reaches us, and that we finally construct our awareness from this heavily filtered input. The "shutting-down" form of meditation can be compared to taking a vacation. We often leave a situation to "get out of our rut." When we return we see things differently.

The meditation exercises can be seen as attempts to alter the selective and limited nature of our awareness, to change the habitual way in which we respond to the external world. In physiological terms it might involve a reduction in the efferent modification of input and in the "models" that we usually make of the external world.

Another form of these meditation exercises consists in the active practice of "opening-up" awareness. *Shikan-taza* in Zen is one of the most difficult of these exercises. Sufi, Zen, and Yoga followers emphasize the process of self-observation. In some of the traditions specific exercises are performed for the purpose of returning awareness to actions that usually occur "automatically," a practice analogous to "dishabituation."

The third major technique in these systems involves renunciation and detachment from "worldly" pleasures. Detachment can affect awareness by removing one of the components that serve to tune awareness: our needs and desires. By removing our needs with their biasing function, our awareness can be more like a mirror.

The second function of renunciation involves the consideration that many of our ordinary pursuits are attempts to reach a state similar to that produced by the practice of meditation. Dangerous sports, sex, food, art, etc., at their best moments, produce a state in which we exist just then, totally in the moment, devoid of our automatic way of responding. This has been termed a state of increased receptivity or expended awareness.*

The problem of reaching this state in the usual way, say the spokesmen of the disciplines of meditation, is that ordinary means are inefficient, that men usually concern themselves with irrelevant dimensions, that the subjective state desired is not often produced by the ordinary means themselves, and that, if produced, its aftereffects do not persist.

Detachment can be seen, then, as an attempt to reach a similar state *within* by separating the state itself from the stimuli that usually trigger it, and by the conjoint practice of concentrating on the parts of the nervous system that produce this experience. These exercises, the centers upon which one concentrates, the *chakra* and the *lataif* in the Yoga and Sufi traditions, can be considered as techniques for inducing a state in the nervous system similar to that which may be transiently produced by external means.

The attempt in these two chapters has been to begin the process of extracting the psychological aspects of these Eastern meditative disciplines. No attempt has been made to provide an airtight case sealed by relevant experiments

---

Within psychology this state is not well defined as yet. It is hardly clear whether "being like a mirror" involves an actual increase in the amount of information that reaches awareness, or whether it involves a leveling of the normal filtering processes — letting no more information into awareness, but simply letting the same amount in with less bias. The only evidence on this question so far is that relating to the brain response of meditators to quite simple stimulation. It will be necessary to extend these studies to get a measure of the "channel capacity" within and across sensory modalities, before, during, and after meditation, and, perhaps, to follow practitioners longitudinally as they progress in meditation training.

at each point. But we may begin most usefully by the simple process of translating the metaphors of the esoteric traditions into those of contemporary psychology and physiology, and noting the overlap.

Chapter Three :

An Extended Concept
of Human Capacities

In this chapter we shall shift our focus on the relation of concentrative meditation to other aspects of the esoteric disciplines. In accounts of the esoteric psychologies we read of "fantastic" examples of alteration in the activities of the "involuntary" nervous system. Yoga masters, for instance, are said to stop or at least to drastically lower their breathing rate and oxygen consumption, to stop blood flowing from a cut, to raise body heat even on cold nights high up in the mountains of Tibet.

We tend not to investigate these "fantastic" and at this point scientifically unstudied claims because they involve that portion of our nervous system which we generally consider to be beyond volition. The philosophical line of thought from Plato to Descartes has emphasized a split of human nature into two distinct parts, mind and body. The "mind," through reason, will, thought, has been interpreted as involving volition — consideration of an alternate course of action, movement of the skeletal muscles, etc. The "body" has been considered as an "automation," going on about its processes, making adjustments automatically. If the name of a process is "autonomic," we obviously do not expect it to be subject to high-level control or alteration. These very terms given to the "lower" nervous systems — "autonomic," "involuntary," "vegetative" — have essentially ruled out inquiry into any possible conscious alteration. So, for instance, the claims of yogis seem so far beyond the realm of possibility, since they involve what we consider to be involuntary processes, that we do not even bother to investigate them.[1]

And yet there are strong indications that Western man's distinctions between voluntary and involuntary components of his constitution are not at all valid. There are other metaphors for considering concentrative meditation that may provide some insight into the relationship of the practices of meditation to the voluntary alteration of physiological processes.

Meditation has been described as a process of calming the ripples on a lake; when calm, the bottom, usually invisible, can be seen. In another metaphor, meditation is likened to the night: stars cannot be seen during the day, their faint points of light overwhelmed by the brilliance of the sun. In this image, meditation is the process of "turning off" the overwhelming competing activity that is the light of the sun, until, late at night, the stars can be seen quite clearly. To one who is limited in his observation of the stars to the daytime the idea that many faint distinct points of light exist and can be seen is obvious nonsense.

That concentrative meditation involves a "turning off" of competing activity does seem quite clear. We recall in Anand's study of Yoga meditation that while in meditation the EEG of the yogins did not show any response to the external world. We also recall that the repetitive stimulation of the ganzfeld and the situation of the stabilized image lead to a state equivalent to that of no external stimulation at all. The repetitive form of meditation is a technique to turn off awareness of the external environment, to enter a state of "darkness" or "void," to turn off the bright light of the sun.

We are generally unaware of many of our internal physiological processes. Our attention is deployed outward, usually for good reasons, for the same reasons that we automatically respond to much of our external environment. It would be quite difficult to behave appropriately if we were continuously aware of every single internal process. We tune out these signals in favor of those impinging upon us from the external environment, which may require immediate action related to survival. Tuning out internal signals is presumably quite an easy process since the signals themselves are more or less constant, and we are quite capable of tuning out the much more irregular familiar signals of the external environment.

The Russian physiologist Bykov, who has extensively studied the relationship between the cerebral cortex (generally considered to process information about the external environment) and the subcortical structures (more involved in internal environment "introception"), makes a similar point: "Thanks to the active state of the cerebral cortex, there constantly arises a functional focus of adaptation which negatively induces the subcortex. As a result of this introception, impulses normally do not reach the sphere of our sensation, remaining presensory." [2]

To return to the daylight and star image, it may be that another function of the repetitive form of meditation is to turn off awareness of the external world, to produce a state of "darkness," to turn down the bright lights of day, this allowing the faint signals to enter into awareness. Our general view of the relationship between the voluntary processes (reason, concept formation, will) and the involuntary processes (emotion, digestion, blood pressure) may be based on a limited observation of the states of the nervous systems, somewhat like watching for the appearance of stars at noon only.

There is no doubt that the "higher" activities occupy our awareness and are under our control most of the time, and that the "autonomic" processes are almost never in awareness and under control. This does not, however, rule out the possibility of bringing the involuntary processes under self-regulation — by bringing the autonomic process into awareness, making unconscious processes conscious. Perhaps the Yoga claim that what we call the autonomic or involuntary system is capable of alteration is not so "fantastic" after all. Careful physiological study of meditators may indicate the dimensions of mastery that we are capable of gaining over our nervous systems.

A review of the physiological studies on meditation and a review of the work of the Russians, especially Bykov, and of the recent, quite precise, and elegant work of Miller, DiCara, and associates, indicates that there is much more voluntary control over our involuntary activity than we had thought possible.

The "trick" discussed in Chapter 1 of controlling awareness by repetitive stimulation and by shutting off external awareness is a well-studied aspect of the control over our nervous system's activity. In the stabilized image situation and the ganzfeld, the appearance of alpha rhythm is found, and awareness of the external environment ceases. In Zen and in yogic meditation, researchers have found similar results: there is an increase in the alpha activity of the brain during meditation. Kasamatsu and Hirai's study on Zen meditation disclosed that the more advanced the practitioner, the more alpha was produced in the meditation exercise. As the meditation of more expert practitioners continued, the frequency of the alpha rhythm slowed down, its amplitude increased, and the alpha began to move from its customary focus in the occipital cortex to the central part of the brain and finally to the frontal area.

Perhaps the most extensive series of studies yet conducted on Zen meditation have been those of the Psychological Institute of Kiyushu University headed by Yoshiharu Akishige.[3] These studies, too, show that the physiological changes occurring during Zen meditation include an increase in the alpha rhythm. They also indicate that it is the "mental attitude" of Zen meditation that correlates with the EEG changes and not the posture of the setting. When the subject assumed the posture of Zen without the "attitude," there was no rise in alpha activity. When the "attitude was set for *Za-Zen*," alpha rhythm appeared in both ordinary postures — sitting in a chair and in *Za-Zen*.

The series of investigations that Bykov and his co-workers began in Russia in 1924 provide evidence that the autonomic nervous system is only *relatively* autonomic and is subject to voluntary control if the situation is set up appropriately. Bykov and his associates used Pavlov's method of the conditioned response. A bell sounds, and this carries with it no special significance to a hungry dog; but if sounding the bell always precedes feeding, the dog will begin to salivate each time the bell sounds. This method of conditioning is often maligned within psychology, since it has led to many analyses of human behavior *exclusively* modeled on the process of conditioning. The unwarranted extension of this method should not, however, deter us from making use of the information available in studies about conditioning. Bykov's studies indicated that, if a process can be conditioned, then it is a modifiable process and, if autonomic processes can be conditioned, they are not really autonomic at all.[4]

Several investigators working in Bykov's laboratory demonstrated that many involuntary processes could be conditioned. Animals could slightly change the level of their body heat as well as the heat in their limbs by changing the blood flow to the limbs, and they could alter their heart rhythms, removing blocks in the electrocardiogram introduced by morphine. The pancreatic secretion could be altered, and the action of the kidneys — urine excretion — raised or lowered. The volume of the blood in the spleen could be changed, the secretion of bile altered, etc. These processes had been considered unalterable. After all, they were part of the "automaton," the body.

The work of the Russians clearly indicates that there is a far greater degree of modifiability of the heart, liver, spleen, kidneys, blood flow, etc. than we normally suppose. It also indicates that the division some have made between mind and body — mind as a process of reason and will and body as an automaton à la Descartes — is foolish and false. As Bykov and Gantt put it: "The gap between the two disconnected worlds of psyche and soma is being bridged." [5]

There are and have been other sources of evidence on this question. The original explorations of Freud and Breuer on hysteria point in the same direction. Their first, quite well-known case cites a woman whose hand was paralyzed. Her paralysis took the shape of a glove, which Freud considered "anatomical nonsense" since the muscles that would have been affected by a "real" paralysis did not stop at the line marked by the glove. Freud's insight was that this paralysis was under the voluntary, although in his terms "unconscious," control of the woman. From this woman's problem and from those of many other of Freud's patients, the concept of psychosomatic medicine was born — a discipline whose very name links the worlds of the mind and the body. Freud's theory was that the woman's paralysis could be cured by bringing this "unconscious control" into her awareness.

So far the work in the discipline of psychosomatic medicine has been limited to removal of misapplications of the latent power that we possess. But there is an important theoretical point for our consideration here. The fact that one can voluntarily bring about a hysterical paralysis in the shape of a glove makes it clear that one can achieve precise control of the blood flow and musculature in quite specific areas of the hand. The yogi's claim to controllability of blood flow and related matters seems much less fantastic. Since Yoga masters spend many years attending to these processes after meditating with the purpose of attempting to alter them, it seems reasonable that, in view of Bykov's work and that of psychosomatic medicine, these alterations can be accomplished.

Certainly the most sophisticated and the most theoretically relevant of recent research in voluntary alteration of physiological processes has been that of Neal Miller and Leo DiCara of Rockefeller University.[6] Their research has been designed explicitly to investigate the possibility that learning may take place in the autonomic nervous system without any involvement of the skeletal musculature. Bykov's work had been limited to classical (involuntary) conditioning, which learning theorists consider an inferior type of learning if compared with that subject to voluntary control (operant conditioning). Bykov's work, as he himself stated, was intended to show that the activity of the autonomic nervous system could always be modified by the central nervous system.

Miller and DiCara's work indicates that the alterations in blood flow, in the activity of internal organs, and with the glands, can be brought about on an operant basis through the type of learning that some psychologists consider to be somewhat "higher." Most important, their research demonstrates that learning can take place within the autonomic nervous system* without involvement of the voluntary skeletal musculature. In most cases, when we try to discover the possibilities of human self-regulation, these academic distinctions may not be very important. Most often it will be of no practical concern whether an action, such as slowing the heart rate, may be accomplished with the involvement of the skeletal muscles or without, but the distinctions are theoretically of great significance because they rule out any possible conception of an autonomic nervous system existing alone.

Miller, DiCara, and their associates studied experimental animals, rats for the most part, in which they could implant electrodes, thermistors, or photocells at specific sites in the stomach, kidney, parts of the cardiovascular system, and the brain. Information about the selected activity in these sites (say, in one instance, blood flow) was converted into electrical stimulation of "rewarding" areas of the brain. (Stimulation of certain areas of the brain has been found to be a reward to most animals.) In order to increase the rate of the electrical brain stimulations the animals were required to alter an aspect of their "autonomic activity" — in this example, blood flow. Miller and DiCara eliminated the possibility of the involvement of the skeletal muscles in this "autonomic" learning by administering to the animals the drug curare, which selectively paralyzes the musculature and allows no central nervous system commands to reach the muscles.

With sensors implanted in specific sites to pick up the signal and information given to the brain in terms of direct brain reward, the animals could learn very easily to alter their flood flow, blood pressure, stomach blood flow, kidney

---

It is almost impossible to rule out central nervous activity completely *even in these quite careful experiments.*

functioning, and the electrical activity of their brain. Miller and DiCara required that differential control over each process be demonstrated — for instance, the raising and lowering of blood flow, the altering of the kidney functions, etc. It would seem that once the information is available to consciousness and the signals can be perceived, many involuntary processes are quite modifiable. The processes controlled can be surprisingly specific. In one experiment sensors were implanted in both ears of a rat and reward was given only when there was a difference in the blood flow of one ear as compared with the other. The rat could not, in this instance, produce the desired results by altering a *general* process, such as an increase in blood flow or an alteration in heart rate. The rat learned to control its blood flow to each ear *differentially*, raising it in one and then in the other.

Another result of the studies of Miller and DiCara relates directly to the aspect of meditation as a process of turning off competing activity, or, in the words of the metaphor, turning off the light of day. When Miller first administered curare to his animals he feared it might slow down their rate of learning to control physiological processes. The reverse turned out to be true. The animals that were paralyzed by curare could learn much more quickly to alter their heart rate, blood flow, kidney functions, etc. Recall that curare is a drug that halts all ordinary movements and the proprioceptive impulses that would normally enter awareness. It may be, then, that curare in these experimental animals performed a function similar to that of meditation in people. Both are means of reducing irrelevant activity, and both may make the detection of faint signals much easier

There is perhaps a way in which our sophisticated technology can help many in our culture to alter voluntarily their nervous system's activity without undertaking a pilgrimage to India. We believe that the practice of meditation turns off irrelevant activity so that faint signals can enter awareness. We may also look at this operation as making conscious unconscious processes. It may be that the old distinctions between mind and body were drawn on the basis of a mere inability to attend to the relevant information.

Keeping our sunlight and stars image in mind, let us consider how we might use technology to amplify the faint signals themselves so that they could be "seen" even in the daytime. If we study meditation physiologically, we can obtain an idea of the limits of voluntary alteration that humans can achieve. Once we decide that it seems desirable to alter a certain process in humans, we can attempt to bring this dimension into awareness through amplification and determine whether it is alterable voluntarily.

For example, one effect of meditation on brain activity is that the alpha rhythm of the EEG is increased. One could build a machine to detect the alpha rhythm and to signal us when we produce it. Such a machine would bring the faint signal (the alpha rhythm) into awareness through a circuitous route. The faint signal would be detected on the top of the skull; the amplified and filtered signal could be converted into a tone, which could then bring the information into awareness. With amplification of faint signals we can be made aware of the periods in which we are producing the alpha rhythm. And since alpha is associated with progress in meditation, this may be a way of receiving information about one of the physiological changes brought about by meditation.

Joe Kamiya of the Langley Porter Neuropsychiatric Institute in San Francisco has shown, with a system that converts the alpha rhythm into sound, that ordinary people can learn quite quickly to alter their brain waves in order to enhance or suppress their alpha rhythms at will.[7] A similar finding has been reported in animals by Miller and by Sterman.[8] These investigators rewarded their animals when they were producing high voltage, low frequency EEG's, similar perhaps to the human alpha, and found that augmentation of the alpha rhythm could be learned. The animals became quiescent and relaxed. Miller reports that the cats sat like sphinxes.

Those who have tried alpha training themselves report a relaxed yet somewhat alert state with attention directed more inward than usual. Subjects in experiments conducted by Nowlis, MacDonald, Kamiya, and my own study in Kamiya's laboratory, tend to describe the state as more "dark," "back in the head," "relaxed," "floating" (compared with non-alpha), all terms that sound somewhat similar to the state of meditation.[9]

Learning to alter the alpha rhythm of the brain seems surprisingly easy. All sixteen of Nowlis's and Kamiya's subjects were able to show some voluntary alteration of their alpha rhythm within fifteen minutes, and twenty-eight of thirty-two of Nowlis's and MacDonald's subjects within only seven minutes. My own study has yielded less striking results — eight of eleven were able to learn a significant differential control in eight hours. The process of physiological feedback as this training is usually termed, consists of creating a connection that did not exist before, amplifying faint signals that are present in the nervous system and bringing them into awareness. Following Kamiya's lead, Joseph Hart of the University of California at Irvine, Charles Tart of the University of California at Davis, B. Brown, and many others have confirmed and extended the work on the voluntary alteration of the brain's electrical activity. Other aspects of the EEG — the beta and theta activity — can also be altered. Once the relevant information is brought into consciousness by technological means, once the stars are made bright, it seems quite easy for us to learn to modify this activity of our brain.*

Out of the increased interest in human consciousness a group of investigators have coalesced around the techniques of physiological feedback. The group consists of psychologists, physiologists, physicists, computer scientists, and many others who joined to form the Biofeedback Society. Their main purpose is to explore the implications of our "new" (old to those of the older meditation traditions) view of our nervous systems, to determine the range of physiological processes that can be

---

Two notes on physiological feedback training:

1. In a sense, the process of physiological feedback can be compared to the use of a bathroom scale, itself a feedback device. If one tries to lose weight, it may not be clear visually whether one is doing the correct thing. It is hard to look at oneself in a mirror and tell whether one weighs 200 or 199 pounds. But the scale can give a more precise indication. If the weight was 200 pounds and is now 199, one should continue doing the same thing and the weight will continue to decrease. In the same way the tone and the scores of physiological feedback devices provide a sensitive indication of quite small alterations, which can be continued and summed up to produce greater changes in physiological processes — e.g., "shaping the behavior."

2. Within psychology the relations between mind and brain have been a major problem. One primary difficulty has been that observations on the physiological end have been restricted to naturally occurring combinations of activity. If we obtain some experimental control over the system at a high level (such as training a specific brain state), we might be able to determine more clearly the relationships between physiology and conscious experience.

voluntarily altered, and to find the most efficient methods of training these alterations, including different varieties of feedback, hypnosis, meditation, etc. Their hope is to bring this extended and more Eastern view of our capabilities into the culture at large. Our technology has been mostly concerned with more and more efficient manipulation of the external environment. That we have been remarkably successful in the past hundred years is beyond doubt. Many of the problems that once plagued man have been solved. Only political considerations, for instance, stop us from feeding and clothing the entire world. We have, however, neglected to turn our technological sophistication inward. We have in general ignored the possibilities of voluntary alteration, which lie within. Our view of our capabilities is now changed largely because of the influence of the disciplines of meditation and the recent quite precise work within science. With this new view of our nervous system we can explore the dimensions of self-regulation that have been the province of a few working in the esoteric traditions, which have not neglected (or forgotten) the possibilities that lie within each of us.

As we have seen, then, our heart's activity can be brought under control; experimental animals can do this, yogis report the ability to do this, and so could ordinary people if they were provided with the proper information. Elmer Green of the Menninger Foundation has presented preliminary data on a yogin who can quite dramatically accelerate or decelerate his heart rate as well as alter his skin temperature.[10] Bernard Engel of the National Institutes of Mental Health has been the first to show that heart rate can be altered voluntarily in normal subjects. He has been able to treat cardiac arrhythmia by the feedback method. Cardiac arrhythmia is a condition in which, as the name implies, the heart beats irregularly. If the patient can simply listen to the irregularity, he can often voluntarily make the heart beat more regularly.[11] David Shapiro and his associates at Harvard University have shown that humans, as well as rats, can alter their blood pressure, given the proper information.[12] If those with high blood pressure could learn to lower it at will, we would have a tremendous reduction in heart disease.

Similarly, Green has shown that a yogi can dramatically alter the temperature in his hand — raising the temperature in one spot while lowering that of another spot a few inches away, producing a separation of 11°F quite quickly.[13] When normal subjects are given information on skin temperature, similar, though not so dramatic, control is possible. (Comparing this with physiological feedback training, if one were to claim control over heart rate, for instance, and demonstrate a rise in heart rate by running up and down a flight of stairs, few would be interested. To take a less extreme example, if one were to speed up heart rate by imagining a stressful situation, or by producing anger, this too would not be of great import.) But what seems to occur is a more *direct* kind of learning — learning to alter the heart rate as one learns to flex a muscle — without meditation.* [14]

The proper kind of physiological feedback training, if the discipline develops the appropriate range of techniques, could simply be prescribed as a drug is today. The advantages are obvious. "Psychologically," the patient would feel that he himself is actively participating in his own improvement. If the patient learns to alter voluntarily the process giving him trouble, then he can, under the doctor's guidance, keep his condition within tolerable limits, and drugs might not be needed. The advantage of

Subjects in Engel's experiments have reported these experiences.

physiological feedback as a therapeutic tool as compared with drugs is obvious. Drugs often do the job that is needed, but their effects persist far longer than necessary, and they often have unwanted side-effects as well. The major alterations brought about by feedback would cease when the training period was terminated and side-effects would be minimized. We should not think, however, that physiological feedback training will be without *some* aftereffects. If any process of the nervous system is altered, there are bound to be compensatory alterations in other processes. The alterations caused by feedback training, though, are likely to be less severe than those caused by drugs. This training would be much more preferable to drugs if it were found that substantial alterations in brain and cardiovascular and muscular activity could be permanently learned.

We know little about feedback training at present. The limits of our voluntary alteration, as well as the aftereffects, are still items for speculation and for further empirical research. However, we do know that, in addition to the brain and heart rate, the galvanic skin response, the muscular tension of certain groups, (the frontalis muscles on the forehead) and the skin temperature are alterable in people. Stoyva and Budzynski at the University of Colorado Medical Center have been investigating the possibility of "deconditioning" or "desensitizing" by feedback. In behavioral psychotherapy, many psychological problems — such as phobias, headaches, and anxiety — are thought of simply as faulty learning.[15] According to this view, a person is simply responding in an inappropriate manner, becoming anxious and increasing muscle tension in a situation that does not call for it. The therapy consists in training a person to relax, instead of tensing, in response to the "threatening" stimulus. Stoyva and Budzynski have used the electromyogram (EMG), which measures muscular tension level, as an indication of relaxation in response to previously threatening stimuli. Their preliminary findings indicate that the process of learning to relax in a situation that previously had elicited anxiety can be greatly speeded up by the use of physiological feedback techniques. If a person can "hear" his own muscle tension and his brain's electrical activity, he can monitor them continuously and keep them more precisely in the desired state. These examples built around current research are an exciting and useful development of science's new view of the nervous system. The focus is still traditional — on removing misapplication of control or correcting problems, functional or organic.

We might also briefly consider some possibilities, more in line with the aims of the disciplines of meditation, of extending the "normal" capacities of man. The implications of the voluntary alteration of physiological processes may lead to an extended conception of the function of education. We might be able, for instance, to learn more precise control over the deployment of our attention. First, simply and obviously, the great increase in the number of students, in larger and larger classes, means less and less individual attention for each student. Computer-assisted instruction is held to be the answer to this problem, but this technique does not take the individual much into account, save perhaps to remember the pace and level of each student. The application of computing machines to teaching has primarily been directed toward the development of very fast capable drill and practice machines. This type of instruction has never tried to take the "state" of the learner into account. While reading, for instance, we have all experienced those times when our attention lapsed and we were "looking" at the pages and nothing was registering in our awareness. At other times we may have been too tense or too preoccupied to "pay attention" to what was presented to us. Physiological feedback training may be of aid here. Suppose that research could delineate certain physiological processes that are associated with, say, efficient verbal information processing. We would then connect the student's nervous system as well as his hands and eyes to the computer teacher, which would make the presentation only if and when the student produces an appropriate pattern of physiological activity. So, in order to see the text, the student would necessarily need to be in a state in which he could read efficiently. If his attention lapsed (and if we could find a pattern of activity that correlated with this) the material would disappear and the student would be made aware immediately that he needed to change his state.

We do not really know at this point whether it is actually possible to determine patterns of physiological activity which unequivocally indicate efficient attention and memory, but this general aim is certainly worth investigating. We have little firm evidence to go on as yet, save the obvious step of working with students who are motivated to learn but who are so tense that they cannot. These students might be trained to produce low levels of muscular tension before they can see the information presented. Allowing a computer-tutor to monitor the physiology of the learner could be one of the possible solutions, and an extremely valuable one to the existing problem of overcrowded schools. It may be possible to train different modes of conceptualization — verbal, logical, spatial, etc. — based on different patterns of brain activity, perhaps taking the brain's lateralization of function into account. The larger import of the newer view of our voluntary capabilities is that the definition of education itself may be broadened. Our teaching is currently limited to the intellectual verbal skills. But if there were objective, easily monitorable, physiological feedback devices generally available, we could include as part of everyone's basic learning experience a training of the ability voluntarily to alter one's own physiological state. We might then learn to relax, to alter our heart's activity, our muscles, and our brains at will. We could, if we wished, alter our awareness; shut it down for a period. The capacities that the meditative disciplines have held to lie within ourselves could become available to many of us.

If the work proceeds at a reasonable rate, this type of training could become a part of every schoolchild's education. He could learn to alter his own physiology as he now learns to manipulate the external environment and receive external information. It is also possible that children who learn at a young age how to alter voluntarily their physiological processes may develop a greater capacity for it than those who learn it at a later age.

These possibilities are still quite remote. All that is known at this moment is that the capacity for voluntary alteration exists and can be exercised using feedback. There is little current knowledge about the long-term effects of this training — whether the physiological definitions of a state of awareness can be consistent enough for enough people to make the techniques useful, and whether the training procedures themselves can have significant long-term effects on the individual. It is far from clear that any of the techniques we discussed before — lowering blood pressure, slowing heart rate, altering the gastrointestinal reactions can actually be applied in therapeutic situations. But it is known for the first time within the scientific community that such therapy may be feasible. And we have, for the first time, developed technological means to make this type of training possible. It should be worth the effort to discover the potential usefulness of these techniques.

To conclude briefly, "forgotten" esoteric disciplines are rich sources of information for contemporary psychology, and a new and extended view of the human capacity is emerging from the blend of contemporary and older psychologies.

Theoretically these older psychologies were the precursors of the modern analyses of the interactive nature of awareness. They also offer alternative conceptual models for human behavior (cf. Gurdjieff's division of man into several "centers" — motion, intellectual, emotional, and the "higher" ones).[16] Their centuries-old non-dualistic approach to mind and body has only recently been accepted by science. They describe an extended set of variables that affect human behavior, which generally are not investigated as part of modern science. These psychologies also offer techniques for altering awareness and the "involuntary" aspects of nervous and glandular activity, which Western science has for a long time ignored. The study of accomplished practitioners of these disciplines may yield a glimpse of the scope of the mastery that may be achieved over these processes.

For the future, once the rich vein has been opened, three major lines of research remain to be fully explored.

1. In the scientific study of meditation and other techniques of the esoteric psychologies, the physiological data gathered so far are quite scanty and the brain changes have been reported in very general terms by individual investigators. We do not know, at this point, how consistent the changes in alpha rhythm are within a session of meditation and across subjects. To say that meditation is "high alpha" is like saying that someone is in New York City. Some information is conveyed, but a large number of questions remain unanswered. We do not know how continuous the alpha is in meditation, or whether there are differences between persons with different EEG's as they practice meditation. Now that computer analysis of EEG signals is possible, we may be able to approach the problem from a quantitative angle. Subtle differences between the patterns of Zen and Yoga meditators may be described and quantified. If people are to be trained to match the EEG patterns of meditators, more quantitative assessments of these patterns are needed.

Studies need to be done on the long-term effects of meditation, on metabolism, on sleep cycles, and on patterns of daily activity. Many of the associated exercises of these disciplines should be investigated physiologically. So far there have been only a few studies on the physiological effects of the Yoga breathing exercises and the *asanas*. Behanan reports that some subjects show increased oxygen consumption in certain exercises, but again, as in the case of activity, more modern techniques may allow a quantitative look at basal metabolic rate, carbon dioxide output, and oxygen consumption. One interesting line of investigation may be that of breathing techniques that may differentially innervate each hemisphere of the brain. One Yoga exercise involves breathing in and out of one nostril or the other. Since the olfactory nerve enters directly and bilaterally into the brain, this technique may have its effects on separate halves of the brain.* In split-brain patients, Sperry has shown differential effects to the hemispheres of olfactory stimulation, and some of the Yoga breath manipulations may be regarded as attempts to stimulate asymmetrical activity of the brain.

As mentioned in the previous chapter, our knowledge of the effects on awareness of the meditation exercises is

---

This research in progress is primarily that of David Galin of LPNI, with me as a sounding-board and spear carrier.

still imprecise. Some studies of information-processing during and after meditation exercises would be of great interest, and so would studies of the effects of the recent increase of interest in meditation in Western culture. Thus we might be able to determine the type of person likely to adopt meditation and the type of person likely to benefit from it. One possible "use" of meditation may be in the "treatment" of drug abuse. Many of the conventional therapies do not take into account that a reason for the use of drugs is in many the search for extended experiences, and the substitutes for the drug experiences are often turned down as uninteresting by the addict. The practice of meditation may be an effective substitute, since it involves a discipline that strives for altered experiences and does not have the harmful aftereffects of drugs. Benson, for instance, proposes a similar idea, and a project of the University of California at Berkeley, headed by Dr. William Soskin, is working along these lines.[17]

The Sufis make use of healing techniques that have not yet been investigated by scientific methods, if they are indeed approachable by science.[18] Studies of these kinds of techniques may yield an extended view of the potential of certain medical therapies.

2. In this chapter we've discussed at length physiological feedback. It is a blend of an older conception of the capabilities of man and of technical innovations to allow some of these capabilities to be exercised quickly by many within our own culture, and perhaps to speed up training in these "ineffable" non-verbal learning situations. Feedback training draws on the older traditions of meditation as well as on the rich literature of autogenic training and hypnosis. Further research will determine the most efficient methods of training in self-regulation, the suitability of different training procedures for different individual, and their most useful application to therapy, education, and the culture at large.

3. The older traditions hold that man is subject to influences from sources other than those which are usually considered within science at present. But there are sketchy indications within science that are beginning to show man's sensitivity to other orders of variables. The rotation of the earth and of other celestial bodies has influence on physiological processes (usually called "biological clocks") in animals and in man.[19] Electromagnetic energy in the visible spectrum has been found in the brain of mammals.[20] The ionization of the air has effect on the ciliary action and is reported to affect sinus activity and healing.[21] Perhaps it might be profitable to devote serious attention to these sources of stimulation (and others, such as radioactivity and earth magnetic field) and their effects on human physiology and behavior.

Chapter Four :

A Closing Note

Man's search for knowledge about himself has been carried out in two modes, the empirical-experiental in the East, and the empirical-experimental in the West. For the first time a blend of the two great traditions of human inquiry may be possible. Some of the new techniques may enable the latent capacities of man to be developed more efficiently and by many more people in the two worlds.

We should note, however, that Western science, as yet, has little or no understanding of the conditions under which these capacities are to be exercised. The techniques and experiments discussed in this book merely serve to modify and — hopefully — to extend our idea of the limits of the capacities of man. Beyond these lie much more radical possibilities, which these traditions also hold to exist — on the physical or non-physical nature of consciousness, on the possibility of "extra," "quasi," or "neo" sensory perception, for example. These capacities are held to be an integral part of an entire body of knowledge (or elements of a higher technology). Many of the writers of the esoteric traditions stress that the use of these capacities must be restricted to the proper time and place. Perhaps these matters should first be explored with those of the traditions themselves in order to gain the particular kind of knowledge that would enable us to put the techniques and methods of science to more efficient use.

Notes

1. The quotation on p. iii: Roger Sperry, "A Revised Concept of Consciousness," *Psychological Review, 76* (1969): 532-36.

Introduction

1. This quotation and several others of interest are contained in an article by Lawrence Le Shan, "Physicists and Mysticism: Similarities in World View," *Journal of Transpersonal Psychology*, Fall 1969.

2. Idries Shah, *The Way of the Sufi* (London: Octagon Press, 2004).

Chapter 1

1. Philip Kapleau, ed., *The Three Pillars of Zen: Teaching, Practice and Enlightenment* (Anchor: Rev Expedition, 1989).

2. Walpola Rahula, *What the Buddha Taught* (New York: Grove Press, First Evergreen edition, 2nd edition, 1974).

3. Yasutani Roshi, quoted in Kapleau, *op. cit.*

4. B. Anand, G. Chhina, and B. Singh, "Some Aspects of Electroencephalographic Studies in Yogis," *Electroencephalography and Clinical Neurophysiology, 13* (1961): 452-456. Reprinted in C. Tart, *Altered States of*

Consciousness (New York: John Wiley & Sons, 1969).

5. Rammamurti Mishra M.D., and Shri Brahmananda Sarasvati *Fundamentals of Yoga* (3 Rivers Press, 2nd edition, 1987).

6. *Ibid.*

7. Frederick Spiegelberg, *Spiritual Practices of India* (New York: Kessinger Publishing, 2006).

8. Ajit Mookerjee, *Tantra Art: Its Philosophy and Physics* (Paris: Ruapa and Company in collaboration with Ravi Kumar, 1994)

9. P. D. Ouspensky, *In Search of the Miraculous* (New York: Anchor Books, 1971)

10. Roy W. Davidson, *Documents on Contemporary Dervish Communities* (London: Octagon Press, 1990).

11. Idries Shah, *Oriental Magic* (London: Octagon Press, 1992).

12. T. Pauwels, *Gurdjieff* (London: Times Press, 1964).

13. See Idries Shah, *The Exploits of the Incomparable Mulla Nasrudin* (London: Octagon Press, 1983).

14. Arthur Deikman, "Deautomatization and the Mystic Experience," *Psychiatry, 29* (1966): 324-38. Reprinted in Tart, supra note 4.

15. See Idries Shah, *The Sufis* (New York: Anchor Books, 1971 and London: Octagon Press, 1964).

16. Vladimir Lindenberg, *Meditation and Mankind* (London: Rider & Co., 1959).

17. cf. Idries Shah, *Caravan of Dreams* (London: Octagon Press, 1995). See the Introduction to "The Magic Horse."

18. R. M. Pritchard, "Stabilized Images on the Retina," *Scientific American,* June 1961.

19. D. Lehmann, G. W. Beeler, and D. H. Fender, "EEG Responses During the Observation of Stabilized and Normal Retinal Images," *Electroencephalography and Clinical Neurophysiology, 22* (1967): 136-42.

20. W. Cohen, "Spatial and Textural Characteristics of the Ganzfeld," *American Journal of Psychology, 70* (1957): 403-410; W. Cohen and T. C. Cadwallader, "Cessation of Visual Experience under Prolonged Uniform Visual Stimulation," *American Psychologist, 13* (1958): 410 (Abstract).

21. J. E. Hochberg, W. Triebel, and G. Seaman, "Color Adaptation under Conditions of Homogeneous Visual Stimulation (Ganzfeld)," *Journal of Experimental Psychology, 41* (1951): 153-59.

22. D. T. Tepas, "The Electrophysiological Correlates of Vision in a Uniform Field," M. A. Whitcomb, ed., *Visual Problems of the Armed Forces* (Washington: National Academy of Science, National Research Council, 1962), pp. 21-25.

23. B. Bagchi and M. Wenger, "Electrophysiological Correlates on Some Yogi Exercises," *Electroencephalography and Clinical Neurophysiology, Suppl. No. 7* (1957): 132-49.

24. Anand, Chhina, and Singh, op. cit. Also their "Studies on Shri Ramanada Yogi during His Stay in an Airtight Box," *Indian Journal of Medical Research, 49* (1961): 82-89.

25. A. Kasamatsu and T. Hirai, "An Elecroencephalographic Study Zen Meditation (Za-Zen)," *Folia Psychiatria et Neurologia Japonica, 20* (1966): 315-36. Reprinted in Tart, supra, note 4.

26. Yoshiharu Akishige, "Psychological Studies on Zen," *Bulletin of the Faculty of Literature of Kyushu University, Japan, No. V* (1968). Dr. Akishige can be written to c/o The Zen Institute, Komazawa University, Komazawa 1, Setagaya-Ku, Tokyo, Japan.

27. Quoted in Deikman, *op. cit.*

28. See Arthur Koestler, *The Lotus and the Robot* (Colophon Books, 1966).

29. A. Dalal and T. Barber, "Yoga, Yoga Feasts, and Hypnosis in the Light of Empirical Research," *American Journal of Clinical Hypnosis, 11* (1969): 155-66.

Chapter 2

1. Aldous Huxley, *The Doors of Perception and Heaven and Hell* (New York: Harper Perennial Modern Classics, 2004)

2. J. Y. Lettvin, H. R. Maturana, W. S. McCulloch, and W. H. Pitts, "What the Frog's Eye Tells the Frog's Brain," *Proceedings of the Institute of Radio Engineers, 47* (1959): 1940-51.

3. Jerome Bruner, "On Perceptual Readiness," *Psychological Review, 64* (1957): 123-52.

4. Karl H. Pribram, "The Neurophysiology of Remembering," *Scientific American*, January 1969, pp. 73-86.

5. Charles Furst, "Automatization of Visual Attention," *Perception and Psychophysics* (1971).

6. For a development of this idea, see Y. N. Sokolov, *Perception and the Conditioned Reflex* (London: Pergamon, 1960).

7. Bruner, *op. cit.*

8. See Walter Mischel, *Personality & Assessment* (New York: Lawrence Erlbaum, 1996)

9. Bruner, *op. cit.*

10. *Ibid.*

11. W. H. Ittleson and F. P. Kirkpatrick, "Experiments in Perception," *Scientific American,* August 1951.

12. George Kelly, *The Psychology of Personal Constructs, Vols. 1 and 2* (New York: Norton, 1963).

13. Robert E. Ornstein, *On the Experience of Time* (Westview Press, 1987).

14. E. K. Sadalla, (Ph.D. diss., Stanford University, 1970).

15. D. N. Spinelli and K. H. Pribram, "Changes in Visual Recovery Functions and Unit Activity Produced by Frontal and Temporal Cortex Stimulation," *Electroencephalography and Clinical Neurophysiology, 22* (1967): 143-49.

16. Roger W. Sperry, "Neurology and the Mind-Brain Problem," *American Scientist, 40* (1951): 291-312.

17. W. Penfield and L. Roberts, *Speech and Brain Mechanism* (Holiday House, 1972)

18. For current psychology's most sophisticated account on the "constructive" nature of awareness, see Ulric Neisser, *Cognitive Psychology* (New York: Appleton-Century-Crofts, 1967).

19. William James, *The Principles of Psychology, Volumes 1 and 2* (Cosimo Classics, 2007).

20. *Ibid.*

21. See Idries Shah, *The Way of the Sufi, Caravan of Dreams*, and *The Exploits of the Incomparable Mulla Nasrudin*.

22. K. Walker, *A Study of Gurdjieff's Teachings* (S Weiser, 1974).

23. Arthur Deikman, "Experimental Meditation," *Journal of Nervous and Mental Disease, 136* (1963) 329-43. Reprinted in Tart, supra Ch. 2, note 4. Also, A. Deikman, "Implications of Experimentally Produced Contemplative Meditation," *Journal of Nervous and Mental Disease, 142* (1966): 101-116.

24. Quoted in Deikman, "Deautomatization and the Mystic Experience." *op. cit.*

25. Y. N. Sokolov, ***Perception and the Conditioned Reflex*** (New York: Macmillan Co., 1963).

26. Anand, Chhina, and Singh, *op. cit.*

27. Kasamatsu and Hirai, *op. cit.*

28. Quoted in Kapleau, *op. cit.*

29. Rahula, *op. cit.*

30. Spiegelberg, *op. cit.*

31. Walker, *op. cit.*

32. Rafael Lefort, ***The Teachers of Gurdjieff*** (Malor Books, 1998, 2008).

33. K Hulme, ***Undiscovered Country*** (Boston: Atlantic-Little, Brown, 1966).

34. Shah, ***The Way of the Sufi*** (London: Octagon Press, 2004).

35. Doug Robinson, "The Climber as Visionary," ***Ascent, the Sierra Club Mountaineering Journal***, Vol. 64, No. 3, May 1969.

36. Henry Miller, ***Sexus*** (Christian Bourgois, 1995); also, Lawrence Durrell, ed., ***The Henry Miller Reader*** (New York: New Directions, 1959).

37. Henry Miller, ***The World of Sex,*** rev. ed. (Star, 1977); also, Durrell, *op. cit.*

38. Henry Miller, "Creative Death: An Essay," ***The Henry Miller Reader,*** ed. Lawrence Durrell.

39. See Shah, ***The Sufis.***

40. For a full discussion of the science of electrical brain stimulation, see Jose Delgado, ***Physical Control of the Mind:***

Toward a Psychocivilized Society (New York: Harper & Row, 1971).

41. For experiments related to these considerations, see W. Wyrwicka and M. B. Sterman, "Instrumental Conditioning of Sensorimotor Cortex EEG Spradles in the Walking Cat," *Physiology and Behavior,* **3** (1968): 703-707.

Chapter 3

1. Dalal and Barber, *op. cit.*

2. K. M. Bykov and W. H. Gantt, *The Cerebral Cortex and the Internal Organs* (New York: Chemical Publishing Co., 1957).

3. Akishige, *op. cit.*

4. Bykov and Gantt, *op. cit.*

5. *Ibid.*

6. Neal Miller, "Learning of Visceral and Glandular Responses," *Science,* **163** (1969): 434-45. Leo DiCara, "Learning in the Autonomic Nervous System," *Scientific American,* January 1970, pp. 30-39.

7. J. Kamiya, "Conscious Control of Brain Waves," *Psychology Today,* **1** (1968): 57-60.

8. Miller, *op. cit.* Wyrwicka and Sterman, *op. cit.*

9. D. P. Nowlis and J. Kamiya, "The Control of Electroencephalographic Alpha Rhythms through Auditory Feedback and the Associated Mental Activity," *Psychophysiology, Vol. 6, No. 4* (1970), pp. 476-84; D. P. Nowlis and H. MacDonald, "Rapidly Developed Control of EEG Alpha Rhythms Through Feedback Training with Reports of Associated Mental Activities" (Stanford, Calif.: Stanford University Press, 1970).

10. Elmer Green, Reported at the Conference on Voluntary Control of Consciousness, Council Grove, 1970.

11. B. T. Engel and S. P. Hansen, "Operant Conditioning of Heart Rate Slowing," *Psychophysiology, 3* (1966): 176-87.

12. D. Shapiro, B. Tursky, E. Gershon, and M. Stein, "Efforts of Feedback Reinforcement on the Control of Human Systolic Blood Pressure," *Science, 163* (1969): 588-90.

13. Green, *op. cit.*

14. B. T. Engel, Presentation at the Society for Psychophysiology Research, Monterey, Calif., 1969.

15. Thomas H. Budzynski, Johann Stoyva, and Charles Adler, "Feedback-Induced Muscle Relaxation: Application to Tension Headaches," *Journal of Behavioral Therapy and Experimental Psychiatry, 1* (1970): 205-211.

16. Walker, *op. cit.*

17. H. Benson, "Yoga for Drug Abuse," *The New England Journal of Medicine, 281* (1969): 1133.

18. An example of such techniques would be those of Hallaj described in "Hypnotherapeutic Techniques in a Central European Community," in Davidson, *op. cit.*

19. K. C. Hamner, "Experimental Evidence for the Biological Clock," in J. T. Fraser, ed., *The Voices of Time* (New York: George Braziller, 1966).

20. E. E. Von Bount, M. D. Shepherd, J. R. Wall, W. F. Ganong, and M. T. Clegg, "Penetration of Light into the Brain of Mammals," *Annals of the New York Academy of Sciences, 117* (1964): 217-24.

21. A.H. Frey, "Behavioral Biophysics," *Psychological Bulletin, 63* (1965): 322-37.

22. *Ibid.*

Bibliography

This is a selected bibliography of introductory reading on some of the matters discussed in this book.

Behanan, Koovor T. ***Yoga: A Scientific Evaluation.*** (New York: Dover Publications, 1939).

Journal of Transpersonal Psychology (a publication of the Association for Transpersonal Psychology) carries very good articles on the psychology of mysticism, meditation, physiological feedback, and related matters. The Spring 1970 issue contains an excellent bibliography on meditation, compiled by Beverly Timmons.

Kapleau, Philip, ed. ***The Three Pillars of Zen: Teaching, Practice, Enlightenment.*** (Anchor: Rev Expedition, 1989).

Lefort, Raphael. ***The Teachers of Gurdjieff.*** (Malor Books, 1998, 2008).

Luce, Gay. ***Time in the Body.*** (New York: Pantheon Books, 1971).

Ouspensky, P. D. ***In Search of the Miraculous.*** (New York: Harvest/HBJ Book, 2001)

Rahula, Walpola. *What the Buddha Taught.* (New York: Grove Press, 1st Evergreen edition, 1974).

Shah, Idries. *The Sufis.* (Garden City, New York: Anchor Books, 1971 and London: Octagon Press, 1964).

— *Tales of the Dervishes: Teaching Stories of the Sufi Masters over the Past Thousand Years.* (London: Octagon Press, 1993).

Spiegelberg, Frederick. *Spiritual Practices of India.* (New York: Kessinger Publishing, LLC, 2006).

Tiamni, I. K. *The Science of Yoga.* (Wheaton, IL: Quest Books, 1999).

Tart, Charles. *Altered States of Consciousness.* (New York: Harper 3rd edition, 1990). Many of the articles referred to in the Notes are reprinted in this book. An excellent source book.

Underhill, Evelyne. *Practical Mysticism.* (London: Book Jungle, 2007).

Walker, Kenneth. *A Study of Gurdjieff's Teaching.* (London, Jonathan Cape, 1957).

MINDREAL

How the mind creates its own virtual reality

Interspersed with illustrations & segments of

The MindReal Tour
by Ted Dewan

Malor Books, 2008
Clothbound, 174 pages
ISBN 978-1-933779-39-3

This is a book that shows, in simple detail, one of the most startling findings of modern science: **We don't experience the world as it is, but as virtual reality.** And while much of the latest scientific work demonstrates this, as do many of the classical psychological illusions, it is an important meeting point for students of the mind, brain, philosophy and religion because, as we can now see in light of this book, all these disciplines begin at the same place.

"...an excellent read for people who have read Ornstein... for those who haven't, an excellent introduction to his work."
Charles Swencionis, Ph.D., Director of Ph.D. program in Clinical Health Psychology at Ferkauf Graduate School of Psychology and Albert Einstein College of Medicine of Yeshiva University.

"The mind is nothing like what you've been taught to believe. There are many different access routes into it, and understanding its overall simplifications and policies can make you operate better and more effectively manage yourself and your own thought processes, as well as manage other people."
— from *MindReal*

Other Malor Books by ROBERT ORNSTEIN

MULTIMIND
A New Way of Looking at Human Behavior

Malor Books, 2003
Paperback   206 pages
ISBN-10: 1-883536-29-4
ISBN-13: 978-1-883536-29-9

This reprint of Robert Ornstein's classic presents a startling new concept of how the human mind works -- a readable and accessible introduction to the new science of the mind, where different parts of the mind are thought to come to the fore to handle different situations. This means that "we" are not the same person from moment to moment and have different memories and abilities in different situations.

> "If there is one book to read on the nature of the human mind, this is it!"
>
> — *Paul Ehrlich, Professor of Biology, Stanford University*

"Robert Ornstein has always been on the frontier of new, speculative thinking about the workings of the mind which has recently given us so many provocative insights. But he has another quality too: he can describe these ideas so that people without scientific training can grasp them...
And now, in this book, I begin to glimpse the implications of seeing our minds as 'multi-minds.'
Professor Ornstein, no narrow specialist, uses literature, myth, and poetry, not to mention jokes, to illustrate his ideas, so this book is not only informative but entertaining as well."
— *Doris Lessing*